The twentieth century has seen biology come of age as a conceptual and quantitative science. Major functional phenomena rather than catalogues of animals and plants comprise the core of MODERN BIOLOGY; such heretofore seemingly unrelated fields as cytology, biochemistry, and genetics are now being unified into a common framework at the molecular level.

The purpose of this Series is to introduce the beginning student in college biology—as well as the gifted high school student and all interested readers—both to the concepts unifying the fields of biology and to the diversity of facts that give the entire field its unique texture. Each book in the Series is an introduction to one of the major foundation stones in the mosaic. Taken together, they provide an integration of the general and the comparative, the cellular and the organismic, the animal and the plant, the structural and the functional—in sum, a solid overview of the dynamic science that is MODERN BIOLOGY.

MODERN BIOLOGY SERIES

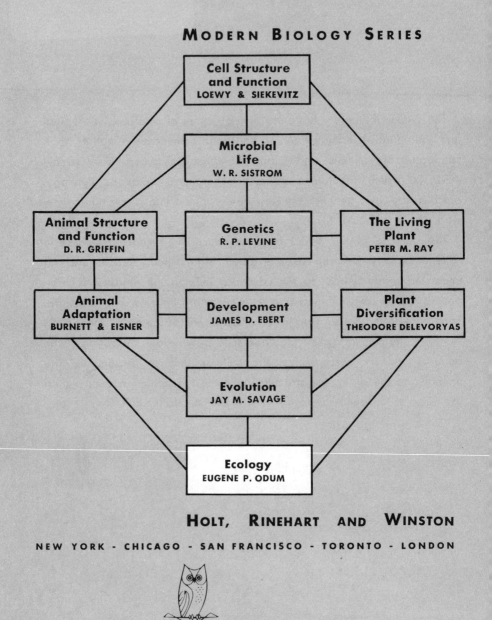

Cell Structure and Function
LOEWY & SIEKEVITZ

Microbial Life
W. R. SISTROM

Animal Structure and Function
D. R. GRIFFIN

Genetics
R. P. LEVINE

The Living Plant
PETER M. RAY

Animal Adaptation
BURNETT & EISNER

Development
JAMES D. EBERT

Plant Diversification
THEODORE DELEVORYAS

Evolution
JAY M. SAVAGE

Ecology
EUGENE P. ODUM

HOLT, RINEHART AND WINSTON

NEW YORK - CHICAGO - SAN FRANCISCO - TORONTO - LONDON

ECOLOGY

EUGENE P. ODUM

THE UNIVERSITY OF GEORGIA

THIS BOOK IS DEDICATED TO MY FATHER,

the late Howard Washington Odum,

WHOSE LIFE WORKS ON "SOUTHERN REGIONS" AND "AMERICAN
REGIONALISM" EARLY INSPIRED ME TO SEEK MORE HARMONIOUS
RELATIONSHIPS BETWEEN MAN AND NATURE

PREFACE

This book is organized around a series of *pictorial* or *graphic models* that illustrate the principles of ecology that are fundamental to the understanding of the subject by student and layman alike. The pictorial model is especially useful for depicting both structure and function so that relationships between them can be emphasized. Once these relationships have been clarified, I believe the layman will be better equipped to understand, enjoy, and preserve his own environment, while the student who wishes to continue beyond this book can logically proceed to descriptive detail on the one hand and more rigorous mathematical models on the other.

Two other viewpoints underlie the presentation. The concept of levels of organization and the belief that <u>homeostasis</u> and biological regulation are important at ecological as well as at physiological levels are strong undercurrents in the approach adopted. Secondly, man is considered a part of nature in this book; therefore, there is no separate chapter or appendix called "man and nature." The influence of man both *in* and *on* ecological systems is stressed throughout. Likewise, application of basic principles in such efforts of mankind as to increase food production, to avoid pollution, to develop self-contained space craft, and to utilize atomic energy are pointed out even though little detail can be given in so brief a book.

I am indebted first of all to students of the University of Georgia ecology classes of the past 20 years who have served as "guinea pigs" and critics in the development of a functional approach to the teaching of

v

ecology. Also, in illustrating principles I have drawn heavily upon the research of my former graduate students. My staff and students in the marine ecology training program at the Marine Biological Laboratory, Woods Hole, Massachusetts during the summers of 1957 to 1961 were particularly helpful, especially Dr. Richard S. Miller, who has read the final manuscript, and Dr. John H. Ryther.

Above all, I owe a debt to my brother, Howard Thomas Odum, whose ideas and research have so mingled with mine that many concepts herein presented are actually joint contributions. Thus, although he has not read any of the manuscript for this particular work, his influence on it is nonetheless very great.

Finally, I wish to thank the W. B. Saunders Company of Philadelphia for permission to adopt certain features used in my textbook *Fundamentals of Ecology*. It should be emphasized that the present volume is not a watered-down edition of the larger book. Although both books deal with principles developed in a whole-to-the-part progression, the present book is a new creation written in a different manner for a different level of readers.

E.P.O.

Athens, Georgia
February, 1963

CONTENTS

CHAPTER ONE

THE

SCOPE

OF ECOLOGY

The coming of the atomic age has made the already vital subject of environments even more exciting, even more important than was the case prior to World War II. The promise and the threat of atomic energy coupled with the promise and the threat of the human population explosion has thrust environmental problems into the forefront of man's thinking. It is mandatory that every young scientist, and indeed every educated person, acquaint himself with at least the over-all environmental processes and conditions that make possible the very survival, not to mention the prospering, of individual organisms such as ourselves. In a democracy it is not sufficient just to have a few trained persons who understand what it's all about; there must also be an alert citizenry to insist that knowledge, research, and action are properly integrated. It is the aim of this small book to outline those basic principles of environmental biology that are of interest, as well as of vital concern, to all of us. Of course, we also hope that some readers will become sufficiently interested to want to continue beyond the introductory level.

In this day and age of science, students are being bombarded with statements about the great need for trained persons in this or that field. In the environmental field the need might even be said to be desperate, simply because man's power and willingness to alter environments has increased at a greater rate than man's understanding of said environments. Society now asks questions that cannot be adequately answered because of lack of data, and especially because theoretical models are not sufficiently firm to allow predictions that have a reasonable probability of being right. One reads about these questions in the newspapers every day. For example, should certain coastal marshes be filled in or drained to provide house sites, or should the marshes be preserved because they are vital to sea-food production? Or, how much radioactive waste material can be safely discharged into such and such stream? The first question can be answered if we know how much of the food energy required by the fishery actually comes from the marsh. Likewise, knowledge of the fate and biological turnover rate of elements whose radioactive isotopes are present in the wastes would help answer the second question. The point is that these two questions involve principles of *energy flow* and *biogeochemical cycles,* two of the most basic subjects that we shall discuss in later chapters.

One thing is certain. The many new orders of magnitude emerging with the atomic age necessitate new orders of thinking. It is no longer sufficient to progress a few small steps at a time; we may sometimes have to leap forward and come back to fill in the details later. In order to do this, however, we must be on solid theoretical ground before we leap! We cannot afford trial and error procedures in many cases, because many alterations of the environment are not immediately reversible should we discover that the alteration was a mistake. Animals carelessly introduced into new environments may be hard to get rid of after they become pests. The introduction into North America of the English sparrow and starling, not to mention numerous insect pests, comes to mind in this connection. As we shall point out later, firm principles are emerging that can help us reduce future troubles of this sort. The Copperhill Basin in east Tennessee is a good example of a mistake not easily rectified. Many years ago fumes from smelters were allowed to escape and kill all of the forests for many miles around. Although fumes are no longer present, the area remains virtually a complete desert of raw, red gulleys with little plant cover of any kind, even though man has several times attempted to revegetate the area. A place such as Copperhill reminds us that biological components must be combined with sunlight and chemicals in definite proportions according to very definite principles if the environment is to function in a way that makes the continued development of life possible.

Environmental biology is a fascinating subject in its own right even if there were no direct practical applications. Nearly everyone has at least a latent curiosity about and interest in his natural surroundings; many develop these interests into hobbies or avocations that prove intellétually and esthetically satisfying throughout life. Children at one time or another express their interest in the living things they find around them by firing innumerable questions at their parents and teachers; unfortunately, some of the answers they receive are not calculated to promote continued interest. As the young person grows, adaptation to the human aspect of environment requires increasing attention and his interest in "nature" often wanes, at least temporarily. The often incredibly dull courses in biology encountered in schools create active distaste for anything living. At the college age, however, interest in the larger aspects of environment is again awakened. In a very real sense the present book has been written in the hopes of reopening some old doors and perhaps also some new doors leading to the living world that lies around us everywhere.

TERMINOLOGY AND SCOPE OF ECOLOGY

At this point it is important that we backtrack a bit in order to establish points of reference and to define a few basic terms. As with any special area of learning, we need to establish certain concepts that are unique to the subject field; we especially need to make clear the relationship of environmental biology to other fields that are included in the Modern Biology Series. Fortunately, a minimum of technical terms are required for clarity at the introductory level; in many cases everyday words can be used in the technical sense by employing prefixes, adjectives, or modifying devices that make the meaning clear without the need of introducing terms completely new to the student.

The special term for the environmental biology field of interest is *ecology*, a word derived from the Greek root "oikos" meaning "house." Thus, literally, ecology is the study of "houses" or more broadly, "environments." Because ecology is concerned especially with the biology of groups of organisms and with functional processes on the lands, in the oceans, and in fresh waters, it is more in keeping with the modern emphasis to define ecology as the study of the structure and function of nature. It should be thoroughly understood that mankind is a part of nature, since we are using the word nature to include the living world.

Ecology is one of the several basic divisions of biology that is concerned with principles, that is, fundamentals common to all life. Physiology, genetics, embryology (developmental biology), and evolution are examples of other basic divisions that are discussed in other volumes in the Modern Biology Series. One may also divide biology into divisions that deal with the structure, physiology, ecology, etc., of specific kinds of organisms (that is, taxonomic groups). Zoology and botany are large divisions of this type whereas mycology (fungi), entomology (insects), and ornithology (birds), are divisions dealing with more limited groups of organisms. Thus, ecology is a basic division of biology and, as such, is also an integral part of any and all of the divisions dealing with specific taxonomic groups.

Another way to delimit the field of ecology is to consider the concept of *levels of organization*. As shown in Fig. 1-1, we may conveniently visualize a sort of "biological spectrum" something as follows: protoplasm, cells, tissues, organs, organ systems, organisms, populations, communities, ecosystems, and the biosphere. Ecology is concerned largely with the latter four levels, that is, the levels beyond that of the individual organism. In ecology the term *population*, originally coined to denote a group of people, is broadened to include groups of individuals of any one kind of organism. Likewise *community* in the ecological sense (sometimes designated as *biotic com-*

munity) includes all of the populations of a given area. The community and the nonliving environment function together as an *ecological system,* or *ecosystem.* Ecosystem is essentially a somewhat more technical term for "nature" as we have used it in previous discussion. Finally, the portion of the earth in which ecosystems can operate—that is, the biologically inhabited soil, air, and water—is conveniently designated as the *biosphere.*

Some attributes, obviously, become more complex and variable as one proceeds from cells to ecosystems; however, it is an often overlooked fact that other attributes become less complex and less variable as we go from the small to the large unit. The reasons for this are that a certain amount of integration occurs as smaller units function within larger units. For example, the rate of photosynthesis of a whole forest or a whole corn field may be less variable than that of the individual trees or corn plants within the communities, because when one individual or species slows down, another may speed up in a compensatory manner. More specifically we can say that *homeostatic mechanisms,* which we may define as checks and balances (or forces and counterforces) that dampen oscillations, operate all along the line. We are all more or less familiar with homeostasis in the individual, as, for example, the regulatory mechanisms that keep body temperature in man fairly constant despite fluctuations in the environment. Regulatory mechanisms also operate at the population, community, and ecosystem level. For example, we take for granted that the carbon dioxide content of the air remains constant, without realizing, perhaps, that it is the integration of organisms and environment that maintains the steady conditions despite the large volumes of gases that continually enter and leave the air.

Homeostasis at the population level is not always so evident; nevertheless, the size and rate of function of most populations tend to remain within certain limits, not only in mature nature, such as a mature forest where the biological structure buffers the external environment, but even in young nature that is exposed to fluctuating physical conditions. One might suppose that microscopic floating life living in a tidal estuary (that is, the mouth of a river entering the sea) would be completely at the mercy of fluctuations in the physical environment. Yet when an investigator (Patton, *Science,* 134: 1010, 1961) compared population and physical variables (with the aid of computers), he found that the community was over five times more stable than the physical environment, indicating considerable homeostasis where one might least expect it.

Finally, it is important to emphasize that findings at any one level aid in the study of another level, but never completely explain the phenomena occurring at that level. When someone is taking too narrow a view, we may remark that "he cannot see the forest for the trees." Perhaps a better way to illustrate the point is to say that to understand a tree, it is necessary to study both the forest of which it is a part as well as the cells and tissues that are a part of the tree.

PROTOPLASM   CELLS   TISSUES   ORGANS   ORGANISMS   POPULATIONS   COMMUNITIES   ECOSYSTEMS   BIOSPHERE

area of major ecological concern

Fig. 1-1. Successive levels of organization in the cells-to-ecosystem spectrum are shown along the top of the figure and levels of major ecological concern indicated to the right. Different procedures and different tools are needed at the various levels of biological organization, but the discovery of the relation between structure and function is a goal common to all biological research. *Left:* Laboratory investigator using an electron microscope to study cell structure. (USDA photo.) *Center:* Fishery ecology students studying size and composition of a population of trout. (U. S. Department of Interior, Fish and Wildlife Service.) *Right:* Oceanographer lowering special sample device in the study of the sea. (Woods Hole Oceanographic Institution.)

In short, we might view the spectrum in Fig. 1-1 as a continuous scientific front. If we are to advance the whole frontier, we must push equally hard all along the line. Concentrating effort on only one point might produce a breakthrough that may pull up the whole front; but most likely only a "bulge" will result that cannot be extended until knowledge in adjacent levels is also brought forward. As already stressed at the beginning of this chapter, not enough effort lately has been devoted to the levels beyond that of the individual, with the result that mankind knows more about his body than he does about his environment.

Returning to our original definition of ecology, namely, the study of the structure and function of nature, it would be well to point out that until fairly recently the descriptive aspect was largely emphasized. That is to say, ecologists were often content to describe the appearance of nature in terms of organisms and conditions present at a given time. Now, equal emphasis is being placed on how nature functions, and rightly so, because the changing face of nature can never be understood unless her metabolism is also studied. Consideration of function brings the small organisms, which may be inconspicuous but very active, into true perspective with the large organisms, which may be conspicuous but relatively inactive. It is evident that so long as a purely descriptive viewpoint is maintained there is little in common between such structurally diverse organisms as trees, birds, and <u>bacteria</u>. In real life, however, all these are intimately linked functionally in ecological systems according to well-defined laws. Likewise, from a descriptive standpoint, a forest, a stream, and an ocean have very little in common, yet all of these environmental systems function in a similar way.

In the next several chapters, unifying principles that are applicable to nature as a whole will be considered. After that, the major types of ecosystems of the world will be reviewed in order to bring out differences in structure and function, especially as they relate to man's interests.

SUGGESTED READING LIST

BUCHSBAUM, RALPH and BUCHSBAUM, MILDRED, 1958. *Basic ecology.* Pittsburgh, Pa.: The Boxwood Press.

CLARKE, GEORGE L., 1954. *Elements of ecology.* New York: Wiley. Chapter 1.

ELTON, CHARLES, 1933. *The ecology of animals.* London: Methuen. Chapter 1.

ODUM, EUGENE P., 1959. *Fundamentals of ecology,* 2d ed. Philadelphia: Saunders. Chapter 1.

OOSTING, H. J., 1956. *The study of plant communities,* 2d ed. San Francisco: Freeman. Chapter 1.

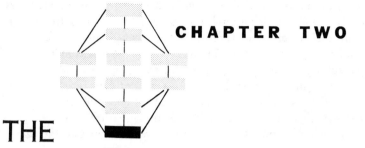

CHAPTER TWO

THE

ECOSYSTEM
As was made clear in the previous chapter, the ecosystem is the basic functional unit with which we must deal since it includes both the organisms and the nonliving environment, each influencing the properties of the other and both necessary for maintenance of life as we have it on the earth. By considering the ecosystem first we are in a very real sense beginning our study of ecology with the gross anatomy and physiology of nature, much as a beginning medical student might begin his study with the gross anatomy and physiology of the human body. Once a clear image of over-all structure and function has been obtained, component parts, such as populations of birds or populations of men, can be considered; or a particular environment, such as an ocean or a desert, can be placed in perspective.

THE COMPONENT PARTS OF AN ECOSYSTEM

When considered from the ecosystem point of view a lake, a forest, or other recognizable unit of nature has two biotic components: an *autotrophic* component (autotrophic means "self-nourishing"), able to fix light energy and manufacture food from simple inorganic substances and, secondly, a *heterotrophic* component (heterotrophic means "other-nourishing"), which utilizes, rearranges, and decomposes the complex materials synthesized by the autotrophs. As shown in Fig. 2-1, these functional components are arranged in overlapping layers with the greatest autotrophic metabolism occurring in the upper stratum where light energy is available, and the most intense heterotrophic activity taking place where organic matter accumulates in the soils and sediments.

From a structural standpoint, it is convenient to recognize four constituents as comprising the ecosystem, as is also shown in Fig. 2-1: (1)

7

abiotic substances, basic elements and compounds of the environment; (2) *producers,* the autotrophic organisms, largely the green plants; (3) the large *consumers* or *macroconsumers,* heterotrophic organisms, chiefly animals, that ingest other organisms or particulate organic matter; (4) the *decomposers* or *microconsumers* (also called saprobes or saprophytes), heterotrophic organisms, chiefly the bacteria and fungi that break down the complex compounds of dead protoplasm, absorb some of the decomposition products, and release simple substances usable by the producers.

The ecosystems illustrated in Fig. 2-1 are the extreme types found in the biosphere, and thus emphasize basic similarities and differences. A terrestrial ecosystem (illustrated by the field shown on the left) and an open-water aquatic system (illustrated by a lake or the sea as shown on the right)

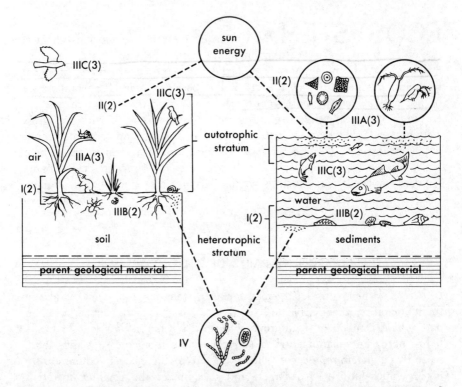

Fig. 2-1. Comparison of the gross structure of a terrestrial ecosystem (a grassland) and an open-water ecosystem (either fresh water or marine). Necessary units for function are: I: Abiotic substances (basic inorganic and organic compounds). II: Producers (vegetation on land, phytoplankton in water). III: Macroconsumers or animals: (A) direct or grazing herbivores (grasshoppers, meadowmice, etc. on land; zooplankton, etc. in water); (B) indirect or detritus-feeding consumers or saprovores (soil invertebrates on land; bottom invertebrates in water); (C) the "top" carnivores (hawks and large fish). IV: Decomposers, bacteria and fungi of decay.

are populated by entirely different kinds of organisms, with the possible exceptions of a few kinds of bacteria that may be able to live permanently in either situation. Yet the same basic ecological components are present and function in much the same manner in both types of ecosystems. On land, the autotrophs are usually large rooted plants, while in deep-water systems the autotrophs are microscopic floating plants called *phytoplankton* (phyto = plant; plankton = floating life). Nevertheless, given the same quantity of light and minerals, the tiny plants are capable of manufacturing as much food in a given period of time as are the large plants. Both types of producers support a similar array of consumers and decomposers. Later we shall consider similarities and differences in land and water ecosystems in more detail.

The structure of an ecosystem needs to be considered from various angles if we are to understand the interplay of structure and function. The producer-consumer arrangement is one kind of structure called *trophic structure* (trophic = food), and each "food" level is known as a *trophic level*. The amount of living material in the different trophic levels or in a component population is known as the *standing crop*, a term that applies equally well to plants or animals. The standing crop can be expressed in terms of the number per unit area or in terms of *biomass*, that is, organism mass. Biomass can be measured as living weight, dry weight, ash-free dry weight, carbon weight, Calories, or any other unit that may be useful for comparative purposes (see Chapter 3). The standing crop not only represents potential energy, but also may be important as a buffer against physical oscillations and as a *habitat*, or living space, for organisms. Thus, the trees in a forest not only represent energy that provides food or fuel but they modify climate and provide shelter for birds or men.

The amount of abiotic materials such as phosphorus, nitrogen, etc., that are present at any given time can be considered as the *standing state* or standing quantity. It is important to distinguish between quantities of materials and organisms present at any one time, or the average over a period of time, and the rate of change in the standing states and standing crops per unit of time. The latter rate functions will be discussed in detail in later chapters after we have considered some other aspects of ecosystem structure in this chapter.

The amount and distribution both of inorganic chemicals and of organic materials present either in the biomass or in the environment are important factors in any ecosystem. We might speak of this as *biochemical structure*. For example, the quantity of chlorophyll per unit area of land or water surface and the quantity of dissolved organic matter in water are two items of great ecological interest, as we shall see. Still another aspect of great importance is the *species structure* of an ecosystem. Species structure includes not only the number and kinds of species present but also the diversity of species—that is, the relationship between species and numbers of individuals or biomass—and the dispersion (spatial arrangement) of individuals of each species that are present in the community.

It should be emphasized that ecosystems may be conceived and studied in various sizes. A small pond, a large lake, a tract of forest, or even a small aquarium can provide a convenient unit of study. As long as the major components are present and operate together to achieve some sort of functional stability, even for only a short time, the entity may be considered an ecosystem. Our biosphere as a whole is actually a series of gradients (mountains to plains, seashore to deep sea, etc.) that are integrated to produce a "chemostat," in that chemical composition of air and water remains remarkably constant for long periods of time. Since the ecosystem is primarily a unit of function, just where one draws a line between one part of the gradient and another is not particularly important. Of course, frequently there are natural breaks in the gradients, which provide convenient and functionally logical boundaries. A lake shore, for example, might be a convenient boundary between two rather different ecosystems, a lake and a forest. The larger and more diverse the ecosystem, the more stable it can be and the more independent (in a relative sense) of adjacent systems it may be. Thus, a whole lake is a more self-contained unit than part of a lake, but we can nevertheless consider, for the purposes of study, a part of a lake as an ecosystem.

SELF-CONTAINED SPACECRAFT AS AN ECOSYSTEM

Perhaps a good way to visualize the ecosystem is to think about space travel. For a short journey, such as a few orbits around the earth, man does not need to take along a self-sustaining ecosystem since sufficient oxygen and food can be stored in the capsule to last for a short time. For a long journey involving a number of astronauts, such as an expedition to one of the planets, man must engineer himself into a more independent ecosystem. Such a *self-contained spacecraft* must include all four of the basic components we have discussed (producers, consumers, decomposers, and abiotic substances) in such proportion and diversity as to maintain a stable environment capable of adjusting to the incoming solar radiation as do the earth's ecosystems. A small capsule with a few components might function outside the biosphere for a short time, but a larger, more diverse system would be more stable and safer for a longer time—if we are to judge from what we observe on earth. Engineers and ecologists who have been thinking about and experimenting with possible space ecosystems have not yet been able to decide on the size and composition of a system that might function completely independent of other ecosystems for the period of time required for a long space journey. The important relation between size of ecosystem and stability will be taken up again in Chapter 6.

As a means of further clarifying ecosystem structure and its general relation to function a more detailed description of a specific aquatic and terrestrial ecosystem here on earth will be helpful.

THE POND AS AN ECOSYSTEM

A pond is a good example of a small ecosystem that exhibits a recognizable unity both in function and in structure. After a number of years of experimentation in the teaching of a beginner's course in environmental biology, I have found that a series of field trips to a small pond provides a good beginning for the "lab" part of the course. Just as the frog is a classical type for the introductory study of the animal organism, so the pond proves to be an excellent type for the beginning study of ecosystems. A small pond "managed" for sport fishing is the best type to start with because the number of species of organisms present is small, but almost any pond, whether fresh-water or marine, will do. The four basic components can be sampled and studied without the beginner becoming lost in too much detail. Furthermore, measurement of oxygen changes over a diurnal cycle provides a ready means of measuring the rate of metabolism and of demonstrating the interaction of autotrophic and heterotrophic components in the ecosystem as a whole.

The "dissecting tools" that the ecologist uses in his study of ponds are shown in Fig. 2-2A, while some of the laboratory apparatus needed for quantitative measurements is shown in Fig. 2-2B. In a class study, students may be grouped into teams, each of which is assigned to the job of sampling a major component or making a key measurement. One team, for example, dissects out the producers by taking a series of water samples with a special sampler that traps, as it were, a column of water at any desired depth (Fig. 2-2A). Back in the laboratory, part of the water samples are centrifuged to concentrate the tiny phytoplankton organisms for microscopic study and counting. Another part of the samples is then passed through a very tight filter that removes all of the organisms (Fig. 2-2A); the filter with the organisms is then placed in acetone to extract the chlorophyll and other pigments. The resulting clear green solution can then be placed in a photoelectric spectrometer (Fig. 2-2B) to determine quantitatively the actual amount of chlorophyll and other pigments. The total quantity of chlorophyll in a water column, or in a community in general on an area basis (that is, per square meter), tends to increase or decrease according to the amount of photosynthesis. Therefore, chlorophyll per square meter (m^2) is an indicator of the food-making potential at a given time, since it adjusts to light,

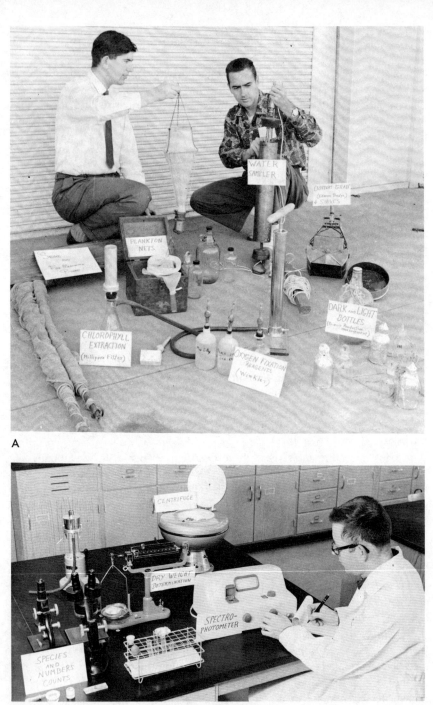

Fig. 2-2. The field and laboratory tools used by an ecology class in the study of pond ecosystem. A: Field equipment including sampling devices for water, chlorophyll, plankton, bottom fauna, and fish together with apparatus for measuring oxygen metabolism of the pond. B: Laboratory apparatus for further study of samples collected in the field.

temperature, and available nutrients. A general model for chlorophyll in ecosystems will be presented later in this chapter. Chlorophyll data can also be used to estimate the living weight or biomass of producers, while the amounts of other pigments tell other stories as will be pointed out in Chapter 6. Thus, the team ends up with four useful bits of information about the producers: numbers, kinds, biomass, and pigment densities. Determining these quantities is the first step in relating biological structure to the functioning of the pond, or to the number of fish one might catch.

Similarly, other teams obtain numbers, kinds, and weights for the consumer groups. *Zooplankton,* which are the small consumers associated with the water column, can be sampled by dragging a plankton net made of very fine-mesh silk through the water, fish can be sampled by seining, and small animals living on and in the bottom sediments can be quantitatively collected with a "grab" built on the principle of a steam shovel (Fig. 2-2A). From these data a picture of the structure of heterotrophic populations is obtained.

The light and dark bottle experiment

Finally, light and dark bottles (shown in the right-hand corner of Fig. 2-2A) are suspended in the pond to measure oxygen changes resulting from the metabolism of the plankton organisms. A portion of a sample of water from each of several levels is placed in glass bottles. One or more bottles are covered with aluminum foil or black tape so that no light can reach the sample; these are called the "dark" bottles, in contrast with the "light" bottles that have no such cover. Other bottles are "fixed" with reagents immediately so that the amount of oxygen in the samples at the beginning of the experiment can be known. Then pairs of light and dark bottles are suspended in the pond at the levels from which the water samples were drawn. At the end of the 24-hour period the string of bottles is removed from the pond and oxygen in each "fixed" by addition of a succession of the three reagents: manganous sulfate, alkaline iodide, and sulfuric acid. This treatment releases elemental iodine in proportion to the oxygen content. The water in the bottles is thus now brown in color; the darker the color the more oxygen. The brown water is then titrated in the laboratory by adding sodium thiosulfate (the "hypo" used to fix photographs) until the color disappears. The volume of sodium thiosulfate needed can be calibrated to indicate the concentration of oxygen in milligrams or milliliters per liter; milligrams per liter is also parts per million, another way in which oxygen content of water is expressed.

The decline of oxygen in the dark bottles indicates the amount of respiration in the water column whereas the oxygen change in the light bottles indicates the net photosynthesis (that is, net result of photosynthesis and respiration); the two quantities added give an estimate of total photosynthesis or total food production for the 24-hour period, since oxygen production by green plants is directly proportional to fixation of light energy. One method of calculating photosynthetic rate of the water column on a square meter basis is to average values for each meter level and convert to oxygen per cubic meter (a simple shift of decimal since milligrams per liter = grams per cubic meter); the values for each meter level when added give an estimate of total oxygen production per square meter of pond surface. In the simplest case, if bottles had been placed at 0.5, 1.5, and 2.5 meters deep then each pair could be considered as sampling the first, second, and third cubic meter; the sum of these would give an estimate for a column 3 meters deep. Alternatively, a graph of bottle values plotted against depth can be constructed and the area under the curve used to estimate the column.

Where phytoplankton density is very low, as in large deep lakes or the open ocean, the sensitivity of the light and dark bottle method can be greatly increased by adding a radioactive carbon tracer to the bottles. After an interval of time the phytoplankton is removed by a filter that is "counted" by a detector to determine the amount of radioactive carbon fixed. This method, which indicates the net photosynthesis, is widely used in oceanographic work. At sea it is not necessary to resuspend bottles in the sea and stand by for 24 hours; the samples can be subjected to the light and temperature conditions of the sea on the deck of the ship as it moves to a new sampling location.

In another approach the whole pond can be considered as a dark and light bottle. If oxygen measurements are made at 2- or 3-hour intervals throughout a 24-hour cycle, a diurnal curve may be plotted that shows rise of oxygen during the day when photosynthesis is occurring and decline during the night when only respiration is occurring. The daytime period is equivalent to the light bottle and the night to the dark bottle. The advantage of this diurnal curve method is that photosynthesis of the whole pond including plants growing on the bottom (which would not be included in bottles) would be estimated. The difficulty is that physical exchange of oxygen between air and water and between water and sediments must be estimated to obtain the correct estimate for oxygen production of plants in the pond. Usually, the bottle methods give a sort of minimum and the diurnal curve a sort of maximum estimate.

The somewhat laborious but tried and true chemical method of estimating oxygen described above may soon be replaced by the "oxygen electrode," which will permit continuous recording of oxygen in a bottle or in a body of water. Such electronic procedures are now in the experimental stage of development. As in any branch of science the development of new methods that increase both the precision and the quantity of data that can be gathered is one of the primary concerns of ecological research.

A SIMPLE TERRESTRIAL ECOSYSTEM

Comparison of the pond with a relatively simple terrestrial eco-system, such as a one-year abandoned crop field or a grassland, brings out other important relations between structure and function at the ecosystem level. In fact, in late summer or early fall a grass- or weed-covered field is an even better place than a pond to start the study of ecology, one reason being that somewhat less elaborate equipment is needed for the "dissection." Since man himself is terrestrial, the field represents the kind of environmental situation of primary concern to him. In a class study of a terrestrial ecosystem it is especially convenient to work with the autotrophic and the heterotrophic strata separately and then to relate the two. Some of the tools needed for the study of the vegetation and its associated animals are shown in Fig. 2-3A, while those needed for studying the soil components are shown in Fig. 2-3B.

Determining the numbers, biomass, and kinds of plants in a field is easier than in a pond. With a class, generally each student removes all plants from one or more locations of known area (a square meter, for example) and places them in a large paper bag. Back in the laboratory the plants are sorted, identified, and placed in a drying oven for later determination of dry weight of the above-ground and underground portions.

The plant data provide a good opportunity to introduce the principles of elementary statistics, a subject the ecologist, or indeed any thoughtful citizen, needs to understand. If we determine the number of grams each square meter sample deviates from the average of all samples, square these deviations, add them up, divide by one less than the number of samples, and take the square root, we have what is known as the *standard deviation*. What we have just said in words can be shown by a simple formula:

$$\text{Standard deviation} = \sqrt{\frac{\Sigma d^2}{n-1}}$$

where Σ = sum of, d = deviation of each sample from the mean, and n = number of samples. Two thirds of the sample values may be expected to fall within one standard deviation on each side of the mean. The standard deviation is a much better measure of the spread of the data than is the range (that is, the difference between the lowest and highest value) since all values, not just the two extreme ones, are considered. For small samples and the kind of data ecologists often have to contend with, the standard deviation can be estimated from the range as follows (see Snedecor, *Statistical Methods*). If the number of samples is near 5, 10, 25, and 100, the standard deviation is estimated by dividing the range by 2, 3, 4, and 5 respectively. Such a procedure is useful only in making quick checks for

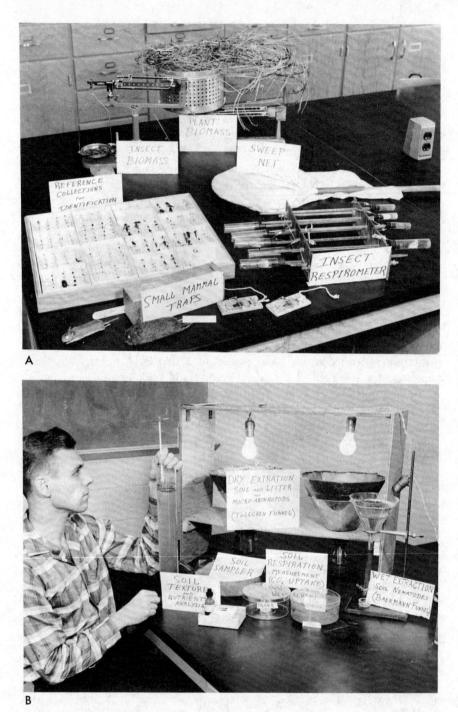

Fig. 2-3. The field and laboratory tools used by an ecology class in the study of an old-field or grassland habitat. A: Equipment for analysis of the autotrophic stratum (vegetation). B: Equipment for study of the heterotrophic stratum (litter and soil).

order of magnitude; it should never replace the actual calculation outlined above.

The standard deviation is the basis most often used for calculation of other useful statistics that enable one to estimate (1) the reliability of a mean, (2) the relative variability of different means, and (3) the probability that two means are different or not. Any elementary book on statistics will explain how these useful calculations are made.

One point always comes out of class calculations: the whole proves less variable than the part; that is, biomass of a whole community is less variable than the biomass of any one component species. The exercises also illustrate the need for obtaining an adequate number of samples before conclusions are made.

Sampling Methods for Consumers

Estimating the numbers and biomass of animals of the autotrophic stratum is, of course, more difficult than estimating the standing crop of plants. Difficulties need not be discouraging but should, instead, present a challenge to the student as well as to the research ecologist. Essentially, three basic methods can be employed in dealing with populations of motile organisms:

1. Total counts from areas of known size
2. Mark and recapture procedures
3. Removal sampling

Since sampling procedures are a problem in most ecological work, the three basic approaches will be discussed briefly. All three methods might, for example, be tried to obtain an estimate of the standing crop of small animals (that is, consumers) living in the above-ground vegetation of our study field. What we shall have to say in the next three paragraphs applies not only to the specific example of the field ecosystem but to ecological sampling procedures generally.

Limited sample areas from which total counts are made are usually known as *quadrats*. The estimate of standing crop of plants, as discussed in the previous paragraphs, was obtained from quadrat data. For the consumer component in the vegetation of the field we might construct a box, cage, or large bag open at the bottom and drop this over a known area of the vegetation. The insects, spiders, and other small animals trapped under the device can be removed in various ways. A light trap or an insect net may be used to remove some of the organisms in living condition; the whole container can then be fumigated with chloroform and the contents of the box removed to the laboratory where animals are then separated from vegetation and debris. Such a box trap method works well for medium-sized and conspicuous species (that is, those easily trapped and readily removed) but is extremely laborious and not too accurate if an estimate of all species is desired. Thus, in an entire afternoon a class might come up with a good estimate (for some species, at least) of the standing crop in only a single square meter, obviously a very small sample in terms of the whole field. The problem in all sampling, in fact, is how best to make a compromise between pinpoint accuracy and adequate total sample size.

In the mark and recapture procedure a sample of animals is captured from a designated area, and the individuals are marked in some manner (as with dye), and released into the populations from which they were temporarily removed. After a period of time, to allow mixing of the marked with the unmarked individuals, a second sample is taken and the number of marked individuals determined. An estimate of the total population may be obtained by the following relationship:

$$\frac{\text{total population number}}{\text{total number marked and released}} = \frac{\text{total number recaptured}}{\text{number marked in recapture sample}}$$

Thus, if 500 individuals had been marked and released, and 500 recaptured, of which 50 proved to be marked, then total number $= 500 \times 500$ divided by $50 = 5000$. Essentially, we are multiplying the recapture ratio of the second sample times the total number in the first sample: $500/50 \times 500 = 5000$. The mark and recapture method works well with those species populations where there is a reasonable certainty that the released individuals will become randomly distributed in the population and will not be subject to different mortality or recapture rates. The method would not be suitable for a quick estimate of the total insect standing crop in a field because of the large number of species and life-history stages that differ in behavior, trapability, etc. Each species, or at least each major family group, would have to be worked on separately. The method works best where the component in question is relatively homogeneous as to taxon, life-history stage, etc.

The third method, that of removal sampling, might be applied to estimating the standing crop of consumers in field vegetation, as follows: A fairly large area, say a rectangle of 100 or more square meters, is roped off. While slowly crisscrossing the area the investigator "sweeps" the vegetation with a stout insect net (called a sweep net); the number of strokes of the net needed to cover the area is noted; the captured invertebrates are placed in a killing jar and labeled "first removal sample." Successive samples are removed in the same manner (with the same number of strokes) and stored separately. Theoretically the number in successive samples will decline as more and more individuals are removed from the sample area. The following are numbers of plant bugs (Hemiptera) removed by successive samples in an actual class test of the removal sweeping method:

sample	number captured	number previously removed
1	115	0
2	67	115
3	42	182
4	27	224
5	18	251
6	16	269
7	10	285

When the number captured is plotted on the y axis of a graph and the number previously removed is plotted on the x axis it will be seen that the points fall approximately along a straight line, indicating that the probability of capture remained constant. If the line is projected to the zero point (indicating theoretical 100 percent removal from the area) an estimate of about 300 individuals is obtained, using the data above. There are a number of mathematical ways of obtaining estimates from data of these sorts but the simple graphic treatment will illustrate the principle. For some species groups in the ecosystem, the points will not fall in a line, indicating that the probability of capture is not constant but changes with successive sweeps. Sometimes the number obtained increases for the first several samples before the decline begins, indicating that individuals become more vulnerable to the net (by moving up from the base of the vegetation, for example) as the investigator continues to disturb the vegetation; in such a case an estimate can be obtained by plotting the final decline line. Sometimes the number falls to almost zero after the first sample, indicating that the remaining animals have dropped to the ground (and hence are no longer sampled by the net) or have moved out of the area; in such cases no good estimate can be made with this method. The great advantage of the removal method is that one learns something about the behavior of different components and is able to judge whether the method is working. Also, once the number of sweeps necessary to sample a square meter has been determined from the removal quadrat, the investigator may sweep the entire field without regard to area covered and thus obtain an estimate from the number of sweeps employed and total catch based on a very large sample size.

The standing crop of other consumers in the field ecosystem can be estimated by one or more of the three basic methods just described, provided a sampling device appropriate for the organisms in question is used. As shown in Fig. 2-3B, special funnels can be employed for small soil animals; in these devices heat or water is used to drive out, or extract, the animals from a given area of soil and litter. Larger consumers can be estimated by removal trapping, as in the case of mice and shrews, or by direct count, as with birds. On the other hand, the decomposer groups cannot be satisfactorily studied by any kind of removal or "dissection." The bacteria and fungi are best evaluated in terms of the metabolism of intact populations.

Some Functional Measurements in a Simple Terrestrial Ecosystem

In sharp contrast to the pond, the net photosynthesis (or net production of organic matter) in a terrestrial community dominated by annual plants can be estimated from the weight of the standing crop of plants plus the weight of the litter (fallen leaves and stems) at the end of the growing season, provided we correct for the estimated consumption by insects and other direct consumers. Knowing the average biomass of consumers and the metabolic rate per unit of biomass (as might be determined with respirometers; see Fig. 2-3A) we can estimate how much of the plant growth was removed. Generally, the net production of an old field is between 200 and 1000 grams of dry matter per growing season (depending on fertility of the site and on the weather), of which only about 10 percent or less is consumed during the growing season. The factors that control the grazing rate on growing plants will be discussed in detail in later chapters.

Direct measurements of metabolic rate of the producers can also be made in the same way as was done in the pond with the dark and light bottle method. In this case the vegetation must be enclosed in dark and in transparent chambers, and the carbon dioxide rather than the oxygen changes measured. Ordinarily, in an elementary class no attempt is made to measure autotrophic metabolism because the technical difficulties are much greater on land than in water. However, measurement of the heterotrophic metabolism in litter and soil can be demonstrated without great difficulty. As shown in Fig. 2-3B, soil or litter can be placed in a plastic box along with a dish of sodium hydroxide, or a segment of intact soil can be so enclosed in the field. Any carbon dioxide evolved will be absorbed as carbonate by the sodium hydroxide. The amount of sodium hydroxide remaining after a period of time can be determined after precipitation of the carbonate as barium carbonate, by a titration procedure similar to that used in oxygen measurement. In this case the amount of carbon dioxide produced is estimated by subtracting the equivalent sodium hydroxide remaining in the soil chamber from the amount in the blank chamber where no carbon dioxide is being added to the air.

The rate of decomposition of specific substrates placed in the ecosystem provides another approach to the study of decomposers. For example, periodic weighing and examination of (1) leaves in bags of nylon net left lying in a natural position in the litter or (2) strips of cellulose placed in the soil, reveal both qualitative and quantitative features of decomposition of plant materials. Furthermore, microscopic examination of such substrates, or cultures made from them, may reveal the kinds of organisms responsible for the observed decomposition. At the research level retention and release of nutrients can be studied if radioactive tracers are biologically incorporated into the original substrate.

A Radioactive Tracer Experiment

A laboratory ecosystem can be set up to demonstrate the tremendous value of radioactive tracers in the study of environments. Several applications have already been mentioned. Just as the microscope extends our power of observation of biological structure, so radioactive tracers extend our powers of observation of biological function. Tagged atoms, as it were, enable us to "see" processes otherwise undetectable by our senses or by ordinary chemical means. In Fig. 2-4 two pairs of dark and light bottles under a floodlight are set up for a tracer experiment. One pair of bottles contains water and a broad-leaved plant, while the other contains an equal weight (biomass) of filamentous algae, thus contrasting the large-type and small-type autotrophs that characterize our biosphere.

With the addition of a double tracer, the behavior of two different substances can be followed simultaneously. Radioactive phosphorus (P^{32}) and radioactive zinc (Zn^{65}) make a good pair. Phosphorus is a major macronutrient (that is, needed in large amounts) and zinc is a micronutrient (that is, essential but needed only in very small amounts). The radioactive isotopes of these two elements emit such different radiations (beta and gamma, respectively) that each can be detected by appropriate instruments. After the tracers have been added to the bottles, very small samples of water are withdrawn at hourly intervals and the sample "counted" (that is, radioactivity in the sample is determined) as a simple means of following the movement of phosphorus and zinc between water and plant. As the tracer passes into the plants the radioactivity of the water decreases in proportion. The experiment ends when equilibrium is reached between water and plant; that is, when there is no further decrease in radioactivity of the water. It should be emphasized that the number of radioactive atoms of phosphorus and zinc introduced is extremely small compared with the number of nonradioactive atoms already in the water and plant.

The tracer experiment illustrates a number of important points in ecology, as, for example (1) the rather different rate of movement of the two elements and the concept of turnover rate (to be discussed in Chapter 4); (2) the effect of photosynthesis and respiration on uptake; (3) the im-

A

B

Fig. 2-4. A: A simple laboratory dark and light bottle set-up for experiments with radio-active tracers. (See text for explanation.) B: A scaler (counter) and two types of detectors, shielded Geiger tube for beta radiation (middle) and shielded well-scintillation crystal (right) for gamma radiation.

portance of surface area; (4) the size-metabolism law (to be discussed in Chapter 3); (5) the limited stability of a small ecosystem; and (6) the very great concentration of nutrients by biomass. The latter phenomenon is of great importance in problems of atomic-waste disposal, one of the primary bottlenecks in man's full-scale use of atomic energy. This area comprises the new subdiscipline, *radiation ecology,* about which we will hear a great deal in the coming generation.

THE CORAL REEF, A VERY COMPLEX ECOSYSTEM

We would do well to close the general discussion of the study of ecosystems with an example that illustrates the value of studying the whole ecosystem as well as the component parts, even when the system is much more complex than a small fish pond or a one-year abandoned field. A coral reef (Fig. 2-5) represents one of the most beautiful and well-adapted ecosystems to be found in the world. Corals are small animals belonging to a group called coelenterates; they secrete around them a hard calcareous skeleton and they have tentacles adapted to seize free-swimming zooplankton in the water. As shown in Fig. 2-5, the animals are closely associated with plants. Embedded in the tissues of the coral, and also in the skeleton, are numerous algae, or primitive green plants. Some years ago Dr. C. M. Yonge and his associates carried out a carefully planned series of experiments with isolated coral colonies in tanks in an effort to clarify the relationship between corals and their contained algae. He found that corals supplied with abundant zooplankton thrived and grew normally when all of the algae were killed (by keeping the colonies in the dark). On the basis of these experiments Yonge tentatively concluded that the algae were not particularly important to the well-being of the coral and its reef-building activities. Some years later (1955) my brother and I were able to measure the metabolism of an intact coral reef in the central Pacific and thus to estimate the amounts of food that corals require. It was soon evident that there were not enough zooplankton in the surrounding infertile oceans to account for the large population and rapid growth of the reef. We suggested, therefore, that the corals in this case must obtain some of their food from the algae. Other investigators became interested in the problem, and have shown by the use of a radioactive carbon tracer that organic substances manufactured by the algae do indeed diffuse to the coelenterate. It has not yet been determined whether these substances are used as food by the coral or serve more as growth promoters. The point to emphasize is that what may be true in an isolated colony in a tank may not be quantitatively true for the coral living in its intact ecosystem where the available energy source may be quantitatively quite different.

	dry wt, g/cm^2	
---	plant	animal
polyp		.021
zooxanthellae	.0038	
filaments	.022	
filaments	.037	
total	.063	.021

polyp zone

skeletal algal layer

fleshy algae on dead skeleton

old skeleton

Fig. 2-5. A coral reef, one of the most complex and productive of natural ecosystems. Upper photo is a general underwater view showing the irregular masses, "heads," and branched, treelike structures produced by corals of different species. What one sees at a distance are the skeletons (often brightly pigmented), embedded in which are thousands of living animals and plants that have created the reef. The inset is a closeup taken at night when tentacles of the individual coral animals or "polyps" are expanded. The diagram is a cross section of a coral head or colony showing the intimate association between the coral animal and several types of algae. (Photographs courtesy of Dr. Carlton Ray, New York Aquarium. Diagram redrawn from H. T. and E. P. Odum, *Ecological Monographs*, Vol. 25, 1955.)

THE AREA-BASED CHLOROPHYLL MODEL

In outlining the pond study it was suggested that the amount of chlorophyll per unit of area might be interesting as an index for the entire ecosystem. This "pigment structure" is worthy of additional attention before we turn to species structure. Fig. 2-6 shows the amount of chlorophyll to be expected per square meter in four types of ecosystems. That all of nature might be included (from the viewpoint of a simplified model) in four basic types of light-adapted communities has been proposed by H. T. Odum, W. McConnell, and W. Abbott (1958). The dots in the diagrams indicate relative concentration of chlorophyll per cell (or per biomass). The relation of total chlorophyll and the photosynthetic rate is also indicated by the grams of organic matter produced per hour by a gram of chlorophyll under the light to which the system is adapted, as shown in the bottom row of numbers. This ratio is often called the *assimilation ratio*. As may be seen in the figure, shade-adapted plants or plant parts tend to have a higher concentration of chlorophyll than light-adapted plants or plant parts, thus enabling them to trap and convert as much scarce light as possible. Consequently, efficiency of light utilization is high in shaded systems, but the photosynthetic yield and the assimilation ratio is low. Algae cultures grown in weak light in the laboratory often become shade adapted. The high efficiency of such shaded systems has been sometimes mistakenly projected to full sunlight condition by those who are enthusiastic about the possibilities of feeding mankind from mass cultures of algae; when light intensity is increased in order to obtain a good yield the efficiency goes down, as with other kinds of plants.

Total chlorophyll is highest in stratified communities such as forests and is generally higher on land than in water. For a given light-adapted system the chlorophyll in the photosynthetic zone self-adjusts to nutrients and other limiting factors. Consequently, if the assimilation ratio and the available light are known, total photosynthesis can be estimated by the relatively simple procedure of measuring area-based chlorophyll. So far such estimations have been especially useful at sea where more direct measurements are prohibitive in cost.

TAXONOMIC COMPONENTS IN THE ECOSYSTEM; THE ECOLOGICAL NICHE

We are all aware that the kinds of organisms to be found in a particular part of the world depend not only on the local conditions of existence—that is, hot or cold, wet or dry—but also on geography. Each major land mass as well as the major oceans have their own special fauna and flora. Thus, we expect to see kangaroos in Australia but not elsewhere; or hummingbirds and cacti in the New World but not in the Old World. The fascinating story of adaptive radiation is considered in more detail in other volumes of the Modern Biology Series that deal with animal and plant diversity. From the standpoint of the over-all structure and function of ecosystems, it is important only that we realize that the biological units

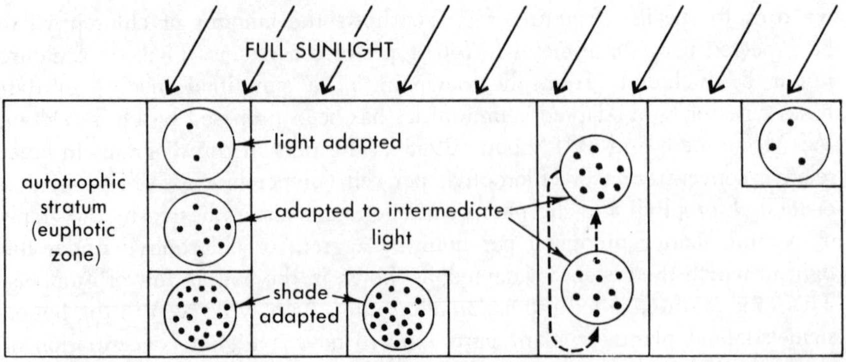

autotrophic stratum (euphotic zone)	← light adapted / ← adapted to intermediate light / ← shade adapted			
Community type	Stratified	Shaded	Mixing	Thin-bright
Examples	Forests; stratified grasslands and croplands	Winter, underwater or cave communities; lab cultures under low light intensity	Phytoplankton in lakes and oceans	Thin vegetation; algae mats on rocks; young crops; lab cultures under intense light (sidelighted)
Chlorophyll: g per square meter	0.4–3.0	0.001–0.5	0.02–1.0	0.01–0.60
Assimilation ratio: $\frac{\text{g } O_2 \text{ produced (per hour)}}{\text{g chlorophyll}}$	0.4–4.0	0.1–1.0	1–10	8–40

Fig. 2-6. The amounts of chlorophyll to be expected in a square meter of four types of communities. The relation of area-based chlorophyll and photosynthetic rate is also indicated by the ratio between chlorophyll and oxygen production. (After H. T. Odum.)

available for incorporation into systems vary with the geographical region. The word *taxa* is a good term to use in this connection when we wish to speak of orders, families, genera, and species without wishing to designate a particular taxonomic category. Thus, we can say that both local environment and geography play a part in determining the taxa of an ecosystem. As we shall discuss later, the biotic community itself plays an important role in determining the kinds as well as the numbers of organisms present.

What is not always so well understood is that ecologically similar, or ecologically equivalent, species have evolved in different parts of the globe where the physical environment is similar. The species of grasses in the temperate, semi-arid part of Australia are largely different from those of a similar climatic region of North America, but they perform the same basic function as producers in the ecosystem. Likewise, the grazing kangaroos of the Australian grasslands are ecological equivalents of the grazing bison (or the cattle that have replaced them) on North American grasslands since they have a similar functional position in the ecosystem in a similar habitat. Ecologists use the term *habitat* to mean the place where an organism lives, and the term *ecological niche* to mean the role that the organism plays in the ecosystem; the habitat is the "address," so to speak, and the niche is the "profession." Thus, we can say that the kangaroo, bison, and cow, although not closely related taxonomically, occupy the same niche when present in grassland ecosystems.

Man, of course, has had a considerable influence on the taxonomic composition of many ecosystems, since he frequently removes or introduces species. We might think of this effect as a sort of ecosystem surgery; sometimes the surgery is planned, but too often it is accidental or inadvertent. Where the alteration involves the replacement of one species with another in the same niche, the over-all effect on the function may not be great. However, in many cases severe imbalances have resulted, often to the detriment of man. The problem has been especially acute in regions such as New Zealand and Hawaii where long isolation has resulted in specialized or primitive taxa. How to predict better the results of ecosystem surgery, and thereby intelligently prescribe or avoid the removal of vital parts or the addition of cancerous parts, is one of the major objectives of ecological research.

It is also true that the same species may function differently—that is, occupy different niches—in different habitats or geographical regions. The case of the coral, as discussed in the previous section, is probably a good illustration. Man, himself, is another good example. In some regions man's food niche is that of a carnivore (meat eater), while in other regions it is that of a herbivore (plant eater); in most cases man is omnivorous (mixed feeder). Man's role in nature, as well as his whole way of life, can be quite different according to the major energy source on which he depends for food.

Species vary, of course, in the breadth of their niche. Nature has its specialists and its generalists. There are insects, for example, that feed only on one special part of one species of plant; other species of insects may be able to live on dozens of different species of plants. Among the algae there are species that can function either as autotrophs or as heterotrophs; other species are obligate autotrophs only. Although more study is needed, it would seem that the specialists are often more efficient in the use of their resources and, therefore, often become very successful (that is, abundant) when their resources are in ample supply. On the other hand, the specialists are more vulnerable to changes, such as might result from marked environmental or biological upheavals. Since the niche of nonspecialized species tends to be broader, they may be more adaptable to changes, even though never so locally abundant. Most natural mature ecosystems seem to have a variety of species including both specialists and generalists.

SPECIES STRUCTURE

In the preceding section we considered the geographical and qualitative aspects of the distribution of taxa in the ecosystem. Now we will take up the quantitative relations between species and individuals as one aspect of species structure. A very characteristic and consistent feature of communities is that they contain *a comparatively few species that are common*—that is, represented by large numbers of individuals or a large biomass —and *a comparatively large number of species that are rare at any given locus in time and space.* A tract of hardwood forest, for example, may contain 50 species of trees of which half a dozen or less account for 90 percent of the timber. A tabulation made by an ecology class in its study of a small area of grassland will illustrate the general picture. As shown in Table 2-1, one species comprised 24 percent, 9 species 84 percent, and the remaining 20 species of grasses and forbs only 16 percent of the total stand of vegetation. Each of the latter species accounted for less than 1 percent of the community. The few common species in a particular community grouping are often called *dominants,* or *ecological dominants,* if we are thinking of ecologi-

TABLE 2-1

Species Structure of the Vegetation of an Ungrazed Tall-Grass Prairie in Oklahoma, Based on 40 One-Square-Meter Quadrat Samples

Species	Percent of stand [a]
Sorghastrum nutans	24
Panicum virgatum	12
Andropogon gerardi	9
Silphium laciniatum	9
Desmanthus illinoensis	6
Bouteloua curtipendula	6
Andropogon scoparius	6
Helianthus maximiliana	6
Schrankia nuttallii	6
20 additional species (less than 1 percent each)	16
Total	100

[a] In terms of percent cover of total of 34 percent area coverage of soil surface by the vegetation. Figures are rounded off to nearest whole number. (Data from Rice, *Ecology,* 33:112, 1952, based on an ecology class study.)

cal groupings rather than taxonomic ones. Ecologists sometimes list the numerous rare species as "incidentals" but this is not a good designation since it suggests that such species are not important. A single rare species, of course, is unimportant in the total standing crop or in the total community metabolism of the moment, but rare species in the aggregate may be very important, especially from the long-term view, as we shall discuss later.

Natural communities contain a tremendous and bewildering number of species, so many in fact that no one has yet identified and catalogued all the species of plants, animals, and microbes to be found in any large area, as for example, a square mile of forest or a square mile of ocean. Fortunately for the ecologist, he can gain considerable understanding of the ecosystem by concentrating on the few ecological dominants with which he can become intimately acquainted. He can also study the fundamental relationships between numbers and kinds without necessarily giving Latin names to all of the kinds. More important, he can study these relationships in favorable places and perhaps deduce principles that will enable him to calculate what he cannot measure directly.

Of course, much of the impressive diversity of species observed as one walks around in the environment is due to variations in physical environment that result in mixtures or gradients. However, even if we select an apparently homogeneous, uniform habitat and restrict ourselves to a limited taxon the same picture emerges. A litter of pine needles under a stand composed of one or two species of pine trees is about as uniform a habitat as one can find in nature. If we were to bring in samples of the pine needles and place them in a Tullgren funnel, as shown in Fig. 2-3, a surprising variety of small animals would be extracted. Table 2-2 shows what two investigators found in the way of oribatid mites in 215 samples of pine litter. Oribatid mites (class Acarina), two of which are shown in Fig. 2-7 to illustrate the variety of form and size, are just one group of small arthropods (or "micro-

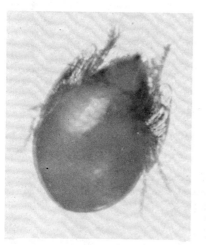

Fig. 2-7. Two species of oribatid mites found in soil and litter, illustrating the diversity of form to be found even within a very limited taxonomic and ecologic compartment. (Photograph by E. F. Menhinick.)

arthropods") that live in forest litter; these mites feed on the dead needles, on fungi, or on each other. As shown in Table 2-2, 60 species were identified among over 6000 adult individuals recovered from the litter samples. Since the species of immature individuals could not be identified, there may have been even more species present. Forty-one percent of the adults belonged to only one species and 72 percent of the total to only 9 species, while 51 species contributed only 28 per cent of the individuals. As in the case of the grassland (Table 2-1), one species was strongly dominant, a small number fairly common, and a large number of species quite rare.

The mite data are treated in another way in Fig. 2-8 so as to place the emphasis on the rare end of the species spectrum. The tall black column on the left shows that about half (nearly 30) of the total species were found in less than 10 of the 215 samples; these are the truly rare species. In contrast, only 5 species occurred in as many as 100 of the samples. When frequency (or number of individuals by classes) is plotted against number of species in the manner shown in Fig. 2-8, a concave or "hollow" curve is characteristic. The shape of this curve is of great interest to ecologists. An unfavorable limiting factor—for example, a prolonged drought—would tend to make the "hollow" curve more symmetrical (as shown by the dotted line in Fig. 2-8); the number (or percent) of less frequent or rare species would be

T A B L E   2 - 2

Numbers of Individuals (Adults) of 60 Species of Oribatid Mites
Recovered from 215 Samples of Pine Litter [a]

Species	Number of specimens	Percent of total	Cumulative percent of total
Oppia translamellata	2725	41.2	41.2
Cultroribula juncata	530	8.0	49.2
Tectocepheus velatus	356	5.4	54.6
Galumna sp.	244	3.7	58.3
Scheloribates sp.	208	3.2	61.5
Trhypochthonius americanus	205	3.1	64.6
Peloribates sp.	179	2.7	67.3
Suctobelba palustris	176	2.7	70.0
Zygoribatula sp.	138	2.1	72.1
Remaining 51 species	1828	27.9	100.0
Total	6589	100.0	

[a] Samples were collected from three stands of pine forest (*P. echinata* and *P. Virginiana*), June 29-August 17, east Tennessee. (Data of Crossley and Bohnsack, *Ecology*, 41:632, 1960.)

reduced, and the relative number (or percent) of frequent species would be greater. Analysis of this sort is useful in a practical way when one wishes to determine if a man-made limiting factor, such as pollution in a stream or a chronic overdose of insecticide in a forest, is affecting the species structure of the ecosystem.

The pattern of a few common species associated with many rare species seems to hold regardless of whether we deal with an ecological category, such as "producers" or "herbivores," or with a taxonomic group, for example, Spermatophyta (seed plants) or Acarina. The total number of species is reduced where conditions of existence are severe (as in the arctic) or the geographical isolation is pronounced (as on an island). Size of organism is important; in general, diversity is greater in small organisms than in large. Thus, we would expect to find more kinds of mites than mammals in a forest. Man, of course, often exerts strong selective pressure as in managed fish ponds or croplands; nevertheless, the pattern of few common–many rare species is evident even in such situations. A well-tended cornfield may at first glance appear to be a one-species culture, but close examination will reveal many other species of small plants, not to mention small animals and bacteria living in and on the soil. Even in the laboratory, a pure (that is, bacteria free) culture of a single species or strain of organism is very difficult to set up, and once established, maintaining it requires the constant attention of the

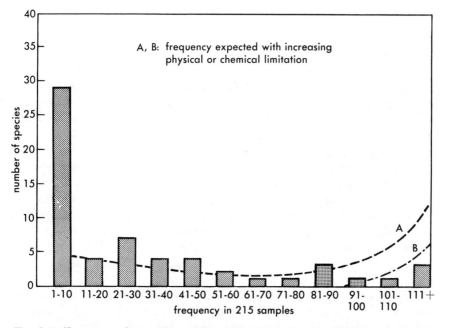

Fig. 2-8. Frequency of occurrence of some 60 species of adult oribatid mites in 215 samples of pine litter in three pine forests in Tennessee.

investigator. Information obtained from pure cultures may be applied to the better understanding of the nutritional and other niche requirements of the species. The species, however, must also be studied as it exists in "real life," since pure culture conditions never exist in nature. We have digressed a bit here in order to re-emphasize what was brought out in Chapter 1; namely, since both the field and the laboratory approach have limitations, they must be combined if the complete truth is to be revealed.

Diversity Indices

Although the pattern of many-species-most-of-which-are-rare seems to be almost an ecological constant (or ecological "consistent"), the actual number of rare species—and hence the total diversity—is quite variable within and between ecosystems, even though we stick to the same taxonomic or ecological grouping. It has been found that if the cumulative number of species is plotted against the logarithm of the individuals counted, something approaching a straight line may result. Or sometimes a plot of cumulative species against square root of individuals is roughly linear. Therefore, we might use the ratios

$$\frac{\text{cumulative number of species}}{\text{log of individuals counted}} \quad \text{or} \quad \frac{\text{cumulative number of species}}{\sqrt{\text{individuals counted}}}$$

as indices to compare species diversity in different ecosystems, or in the same ecosystem at different times (as, for example, before and after pollution). Or at least we could compare the slopes of the graphs to determine where diversity is greatest or least, even if the lines are not straight. Such a comparison is made in Fig. 2-9. In this study large numbers of shells of mollusks were collected from the bottoms of coastal bays at three points in a salinity gradient. Note that the relationships are not strictly straight-line ones, and hence the relationship is affected by the size of sample. Nevertheless, species diversity was definitely greatest in waters of moderate salinity as compared with either extreme hypersaline or hyposaline conditions. In many other situations as well it has been found that *the greatest diversity occurs in the moderate or middle range of a physical gradient.* In the case of the shells, one might infer past environmental conditions by determining the species-numbers relations of buried or fossilized shells of known geological age. This example, by the way, will serve to introduce another interesting aspect of environmental biology, which we call *paleoecology.*

Without going into the mathematics involved in theories of diversity, we will point out that many other types of diversity indices have been proposed. In addition to species-numbers indices that we have been discussing, species-area relationships (that is, number of species per unit of area) are

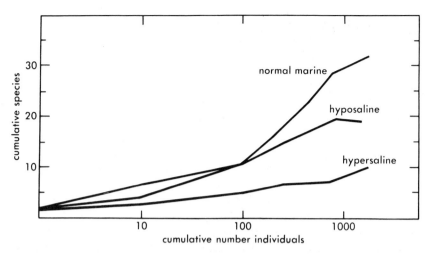

Fig. 2-9. Cumulative number of species plotted against log of cumulative number of individuals in samples of mollusk shells from three Texas bays differing in salinity. The number of species per 1000 individuals was greater at normal salinity of the Gulf of Mexico than in bays with lower or higher salinity. (Redrawn from H. T. Odum, J. E. Cantlon, and L. S. Kornicker, *Ecology*, Vol. 41, 1960.)

equally interesting and important. One bottleneck, as always, is the difficulty of obtaining data that are not biased by sampling techniques.

Population Dispersion

The way in which individuals in a population are dispersed in space is an important aspect of community structure and has considerable bearing on sampling procedures and diversity indices. In general, we may distinguish three broad patterns: (1) *Random* distribution, in which the probability of an individual occurring at any one spot is the same as the probability of its occurring at any other spot. (2) *Uniform* distribution, in which individuals occur more regularly than random, such as corn stalks in a corn field. (3) *Clumped* distribution, in which individuals are more irregular than random; that is, individuals occur in groups, such as a clump of plants arising from vegetative reproduction, or a flock of birds. Groups, of course, can be dispersed randomly, uniformly, or in clumped fashion. Some "lone wolf" predators such as spiders and certain plants show a random distribution in nature, and sometimes individuals approach uniform distribution where they are antagonistic or repel one another in a uniform habitat. Mostly, however, populations show some degree of clumping. Obviously, the greater the clumping the greater the care that must be taken in sampling and in interpreting diversity indices based on samples.

The Importance of Diversity

We may now ask a series of questions that are extremely important to mankind. We will not attempt to answer them in detail now, since we need to build more background in ecological principles; also, we must admit that we cannot (or at least the author cannot) fully answer them anyway. However, we will make a few points for you to think about, and we will come back to this important subject in subsequent chapters. Why are there so many rare species in ecosystems? How are so many species able to survive in such low numbers? What role does the rare species really play in the ecosystem? What difference does it make if there are one or many species in a trophic level? Or, as the practical-minded individual would ask: what good are all those odd species? Since in the aggregate they may occupy considerable room, or compete with common species for resources, why not kill them all off so the few species best adapted and most useful to man can take their place?

It is now generally assumed, but without much real scientific evidence, that the "advantage" of a diversity of species—that is, the survival value to the community—lies in increased stability. The more species present, the greater the possibilities for adaptation to changing conditions, whether these be short-term or long-term changes in climate or other factors. Or to put it another way, the greater the gene pool the greater the adaptation potential. Occurrences in certain areas of Long Island Sound (eastern United States), once a prolific source of oysters, may be an example of an adaptation that would not have been possible if rare species had not been present. The development of large-scale domestic duck farming on shore introduced large amounts of organic manure into the shallow waters. The dominant or abundant phytoplankton producers of these waters were unable to tolerate the changed conditions, but several other species that had formerly been very rare were able to tolerate and exploit the organic materials and soon became very abundant. The productivity of the ecosystem was thus maintained (or actually increased because of the fertilization) because producers were present that could "take over." Unfortunately, in this case, the oysters could not use the new phytoplankton as food and the oyster industry was depressed by the duck industry.

Man should make careful note of the situation in adapted, naturally diverse communities in planning his agricultural ecosystems. It would seem to be most risky for man to depend on only one or a few varieties of wheat or pine trees just because the yield happens to be highest at the moment. Should a sudden disease or climatic change occur, specialized species or varieties could be wiped out.

Above all, the study of ecology suggests that we should have a healthy respect for all forms of life. While the "good guys" and the "bad guys" may be clearly distinguishable on the dramatic stage, such is not the case in real life. Many seemingly useless organisms turn out to be useful. In fact, it is fortunate for man that the biosphere is populated with such a variety of organisms that some of them can tolerate even severe pollution and thus keep a bad situation from becoming worse. There will be more about the critical problem of man-made pollution in Chapter 4.

Man needs to think more in terms of the control and the utilization of nature, and not so much in terms of wholesale extermination, except in the case of a few species that are direct parasites or competitors. *Conservation of the ecosystem* rather than *conservation of this or that species,* as is now the current emphasis, would seem to be the most sensible approach. Until we have real scientific evidence to the contrary, it is clearly in our interest to preserve some of the remarkable diversity of taxa that have developed during the evolution of the biosphere over millions of years. The diversity of life should be looked upon as a national and international treasury.

THE RELATIONSHIPS BETWEEN STRUCTURE AND FUNCTION IN THE ECOSYSTEM

All of the above discussion has been leading up to a single point that is one of the most important in this book. A description of an ecosystem consisting of a list of component species and their distribution and number is not sufficient information in itself to determine how a biotic community works. For a full understanding of nature, *rate functions* must also be investigated. Furthermore, *structure and function are best studied together* as far as is feasible. One reason for being emphatic on this point is that, in traditional biological teaching, it has long been the custom to separate structure and function. Too often the student has been required to study and memorize many details of structure, without any thought as to their function. Perhaps an analogy from the history of biology will be helpful in this connection. The Greeks studied the anatomy of the human heart and circulatory system quite intensively; they knew the gross anatomy quite well. However, their ideas of function, based as they were only on the gross anatomy of the cadaver, were quite wrong. The true nature of blood circulation was not discovered until investigators worked with the living animal and man. Harvey worked out the function even though he did not know about the capillaries; once the correct function was suggested, it was only a matter of time before these small structures were looked for and found. So it is with nature; we need to study function in order to know what structures need restudying, and vice versa.

The relation of function to structure is a central problem at all levels, a fact that is apparent in other books in the Modern Biology Series. Thus, the cell physiologist is not satisfied until he understands how the molecular structure of an enzyme is related to what it does in the cell. Likewise, the ecologist cannot be satisfied until he understands how species structure or trophic structure is related to productivity and stability of the community.

SUGGESTED READING LIST

Cole, Lamont, "The ecosphere," *Scientific American*, April 1958, pp. 83–92.

Elton, Charles S., 1958. *The ecology of invasions by animals and plants.* London: Methuen. Chapters 1, 2, 8, and 9.

Evans, Francis C., "Ecosystem as the basic unit in ecology," *Science*, Vol. 123 (1956), pp. 1127–1128.

Forbes, Stephen A., "The lake as a microcosm." A classic essay written in 1887 and reprinted in *Illinois Natural History Survey Bulletin*, Vol. 15 (1925), p. 537.

Hutchinson, G. E., "Homage to Santa Rosalia or why are there so many kinds of animals?" *American Naturalist*, Vol. 93 (1959), pp. 145–159.

Kohn, Alan J., "The biology of atolls," *Bios*, Vol. 32 (1961), pp. 113–126.

Odum, Eugene P., 1959. *Fundamentals of ecology*, 2d ed. Philadelphia: Saunders. Ecosystem, pp. 10–27; species-numbers, pp. 281–283; structure of aquatic ecosystems, pp. 291–316; structure of terrestrial ecosystems, pp. 368–375.

Odum, Howard T., Cantlon, John E., and Kornicker, Louis S., "An organizational hierarchy postulate for the interpretation of species-individual distributions, species entropy, ecosystem evolution, and the meaning of a species-variety index," *Ecology*, Vol. 41 (1960), pp. 395–399.

———, McConnell, William, and Abbott, Walter, "The chlorophyll 'A' of communities," *Publications of the Institute for Marine Science*, Univ. Texas, Vol. 5 (1958), pp. 65–96.

———, and Odum, E. P., "Trophic structure and productivity of a windward coral reef community on Eniwetok Atoll," *Ecological Monographs*, Vol. 25 (1955), pp. 291–320.

Whittaker, R. H., 1960. "Ecosystem," *McGraw-Hill encyclopedia of science and technology*, Vol. 4, pp. 404-408.

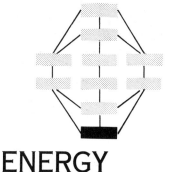

CHAPTER THREE

ENERGY

FLOW

AND NATURE'S

METABOLISM
In the previous chapter we outlined the gross structure of an ecosystem; in this and the next chapter the major principles of gross function will be outlined. We shall then be in a better position to attempt to answer some of the questions raised concerning relationships between structure and function.

ENERGY AND MATERIALS

Assuming that adapted organisms are present in an area of the biosphere, the number of organisms and the rate at which they live depends, in the final analysis, on the rate at which energy flows through the biological part of the system and on the rate at which materials circulate within the system and/or are exchanged with adjacent systems. It is important to emphasize that nonenergy-yielding materials circulate, but energy does not. Nitrogen, carbon, water, and other materials of which living organisms are composed may circulate many times between living and nonliving entities; that is, any given atom of material may be used over and over again. On the other hand, energy is used once by a given organism or population, is converted into heat, and is soon lost from the ecosystem. The food you ate for breakfast is no longer available to you when it has been respired; you must go to the store and buy more for tomorrow. Life (including the inflow of food at the grocery store) is kept going by the continuous inflow of sunlight from the outside.

The one-way flow of energy, as a universal phenomenon in nature, is the result of operation of the laws of thermodynamics, which are fundamental concepts of physics. The first law states, as you may recall, that energy may be transformed from one type (for example, light) into another (for example, potential energy of food) but is never created nor destroyed. The second law of thermodynamics states that no process involving an energy transformation will occur unless there is a degradation of energy from a concentrated form into a dispersed form. Because some energy is always dispersed into unavailable heat energy, no spontaneous transformation (as light to food, for example) can be 100 percent efficient.

The interaction of energy and materials in the ecosystem is of primary concern to ecologists. In fact, it may be said that the *one-way flow of energy* and the *circulation of materials* are the two great principles or "laws" of general ecology, since these principles apply equally to all environments and all organisms including man. In this chapter some aspects of energy flow within the biological components of the ecosystem will be considered; the cycling of materials and the part that the physical environment plays in limiting biological productivity will be discussed in more detail in the next two chapters.

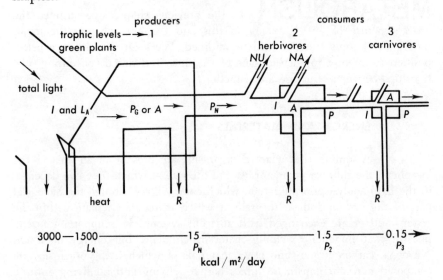

Fig. 3-1. A simplified energy flow diagram. The boxes represent the standing crop of organisms (1: producers or autotrophs; 2: primary consumers or herbivores; 3: secondary consumers or carnivores) and the pipes represent the flow of energy through the biotic community. L = total light; L_A = absorbed light; P_G = gross production; P_N = net production; I = energy intake; A = assimilated energy; NA = non-assimilated energy; NU = unused energy (stored or exported); R = respiratory energy loss. The chain of figures along the lower margin of the diagram indicates the order of magnitude expected at each successive transfer starting with 3000 kcal of incident light per m² per day.

Fig. 3-1 is a simplified energy flow diagram that might, in principle, be applied to any ecosystem. The boxes represent the population mass or biomass, and the pipes depict the flow of energy between the living units. Only about half of the average sunlight impinging upon green plants (that is, producers) is absorbed by the photosynthetic machinery, and only a small portion of absorbed energy—about 1 to 5 percent for productive vegetation—is converted into food energy. The total assimilation rate of producers in an ecosystem is designated as *primary production* or *primary productivity* (P_G or A in Fig. 3-1). It is the total amount of organic matter fixed, including that used up by plant respiration during the measurement period. *Net primary productivity* is the organic matter stored in plant tissues in excess of respiration during the period of measurement. Net production represents food potentially available to heterotrophs. In Fig. 3-1 net primary production is represented by the flow, P, that leaves the producer component. When plants are growing rapidly under favorable light and temperature conditions, plant respiration may account for as little as 10 percent of gross production so that net production may be 90 percent of gross. However, under most conditions in nature net production is a smaller percentage of gross.

FOOD CHAINS AND TROPHIC LEVELS

The transfer of food energy from the source in plants through a series of organisms with repeated stages of eating and being eaten is known as the *food chain*. In complex natural communities, organisms whose food is obtained from plants by the same number of steps are said to belong to the same *trophic level*. Thus, green plants occupy the first trophic level (the producer level), plant eaters (herbivores, etc.) the second level (the primary consumer level), carnivores that eat the herbivores the third level (secondary consumers), and perhaps even a fourth level (tertiary consumers). It should be emphasized that this trophic classification is one of function, and not of species as such; a given species population may occupy one, or more than one, trophic level according to the source of energy actually assimilated. We have already called attention to certain algae that may depend in part on their own food and in part on food made by other algae; or the populations of men who utilize food from both plant and animal sources.

At each transfer of energy from one organism to another, or from one trophic level to another, a large part of the energy is degraded into heat, as required by the second law of thermodynamics. The shorter the food chain, or the nearer the organism to the beginning of the food chain, the greater the available food energy. As shown in Fig. 3-1, the energy flows are greatly reduced with each successive trophic level, whether we consider the total flow (A), or the production (P) or respiration (R) components. Thus, more men can survive on a given square mile if they function as primary rather than secondary consumers.

Approximate quantitative relations to be expected in the energy flow of an ecosystem are shown by the chain of figures along the lower margin of Fig. 3-1. Roughly speaking, the reduction with each transformation (that is, with each link in the food chain) seems to be about two orders of magnitude at the first or primary trophic level, and about one order of magnitude thereafter. By order of magnitude we mean by a factor of 10. If an average of 1500 Calories of light energy were absorbed by green plants per square meter per day (a reasonable amount for the temperate zone), we might expect 15 Calories to end up as net plant production, 1.5 Calories to be reconstituted as primary consumers (herbivores), and 0.15 Calories as secondary consumers (carnivores)—provided, of course, that there are adapted organisms present that can fully utilize these resources. While a small amount of the primary food energy could be involved in a number of transfers, it is evident that the amount of food remaining after two or three successive transfers is so small that few organisms could be supported if they had to depend entirely on food available at the end of a long food chain. For all practical purposes, then, the food chain is limited to three or four "links."

It should be emphasized that the scheme in Fig. 3-1 is a model useful for making comparisons with the real thing. Somewhat larger, and frequently quite a bit smaller, percentages may actually be involved under different conditions. Much remains to be learned, not only about the orders of magnitude in different ecosystems but also about the upper limits. Since the efficiencies of transfer (1 to 10 percent) seem low in terms of man-made machines, man has often thought that he could improve on nature by increasing the percent of transfer of light to food, and food to consumer. Before we can discuss this very important matter, however, we shall need to fill in a bit more background.

At this point it would be well to make clear a few points about units, ratios, and efficiencies. Too often our thinking is clouded by people who, unintentionally or intentionally, use units that are not comparable in forming ratios and percentages. The basic unit of energy most suitable for use in ecology is the large or kilogram Calorie, which is defined as the amount of heat needed to raise one liter (that is, one kilogram) of water one degree centigrade. The small, or gram-calorie (heat needed to raise 1 gram of water 1° C), is also used in work with small organisms or small amounts of energy. In this book we shall use the abbreviation kcal for the large Calorie and cal for the smaller unit. Where caloric value of biomass is uniform, units of weight may be used in describing community energetics. In general, plant biomass runs about 4 kcal per ash-free dry gram, and animal close to 5. Where energy is being stored, as in seeds or in bodies of migrating or hibernating animals, the values approach 7 or 8 kcal. The main point to remember about ratios and percentages when used as estimates of efficiency is that they should be *dimensionless*; that is, the same unit should be used for both the denominator and numerator of the ratio. Thus, it should be Calories/Calories or grams dry weight/grams dry weight, and not calories/pounds. Otherwise comparisons may not be valid. A conversion of 100 pounds of dry corn into 10 pounds of dressed hog meat is not the same efficiency as the conversion of 100 pounds of grass into 10 pounds of cow on the hoof, because the energy value per pound is quite different for the various materials.

THE RELATIONSHIP BETWEEN ENERGY FLOW AND THE STANDING CROP

As already indicated, the boxes in Fig. 3-1 represent the biomass of the standing crop of organisms functioning at the trophic level indicated. The relationship between the "boxes" and the "pipes"—that is, between standing crops and the energy flows P, A, or I—is of great interest and importance. As we have seen, the energy flow must always decrease with each successive trophic level. Likewise, in many situations, the standing crop also decreases (as shown in Fig. 3-1). However, standing crop biomass is much influenced by the size of the individual organisms making up the trophic group in question. In general, the smaller the organism the greater the rate of metabolism per gram of weight. This trend is often known as the *inverse size—metabolic rate* "law". Thus, one gram of small algae may be equal in metabolism to many grams of forest tree leaves. Consequently, if the producers of an ecosystem are composed largely of very small organisms, and the consumers are large, the standing crop biomass of consumers may be greater than that of the producers even though, of course, the energy flow of the latter must average greater (assuming that food used by consumers is not being "imported" from another ecosystem). Such a situation often exists in marine environments where the water is moderately deep: bottom-dwelling invertebrate consumers (clams, crustaceans, echinoderms, etc.) and fish often outweigh the microscopic phytoplankton on which they depend. By harvesting at frequent intervals, man (as well as the clam) may obtain as much food (net production) from mass cultures of small algae as he obtains from a grain crop harvested after a long interval of time. However, the standing crop of algae at any one time would be much less than that of a mature grain crop.

To reiterate, standing crop biomass is usually expressed in terms of grams of organic matter, grams of carbon, or *Calories per unit area* (square meter, hectare, acre, etc.). Productivity is a rate to be expressed as grams or Calories per unit area per unit time. As indicated by the examples, these two quantities should not be confused; the relationship between the two depends on the kind of organisms involved.

PRODUCTION AND UTILIZATION RATES

The relationship between gross production (P_g) and total community respiration (the sum of all R's in Fig. 3-1) is important in the understanding of the total function of the ecosystem and in predicting future events. One kind of ecological "climax" or "steady state" exists if the annual production of organic matter equals total consumption $(P/R = 1)$ and if exports and imports of organic matter are either nonexistent (as in a self-sufficient climax) or equal. In a mature tropical rain forest the balance may be almost a day by day affair, whereas in mature temperate forests an autotrophic regime in summer is balanced by a heterotrophic regime in winter. Another type of steady state exists if gross production plus imports equal total respiration, as in some types of stream ecosystems, or if gross production equals respiration plus exports, as in stable agriculture.

Seasonal fluctuations and annual shifts related to short-term meteorological or other cycles in the physical environment occur in almost all ecosystems, but the over-all structure and species composition of steady-state communities tend to remain the same, although it is not yet certain that this is always true. If primary production and heterotrophic utilization are not equal $(P/R$ greater or less than 1), with the result that organic matter either accumulates or is depleted, we may expect the community to change by the process of *ecological succession*. Succession may proceed either from an extremely autotrophic condition $(P>R)$ or from the extremely heterotrophic condition $(P<R)$ toward a steady-state condition in which P equals R. Organic development in a new pond, or the development of a forest on a fallow field, are examples of the first kind of succession. In these situations the kinds of organisms change rapidly from year to year and organic matter accumulates. Changes in a stream polluted with a large amount of organic sewage is an example of the other type of succession, in which organic matter is used up faster than it is produced. Ecological succession will be discussed in greater detail in Chapter 6.

A Y-SHAPED ENERGY FLOW DIAGRAM AS A WORKING MODEL

As was discussed in the chapter on ecosystems, dividing the heterotrophs into large and small categories—that is, macroconsumers and decomposers—is arbitrary in terms of function but convenient in terms of

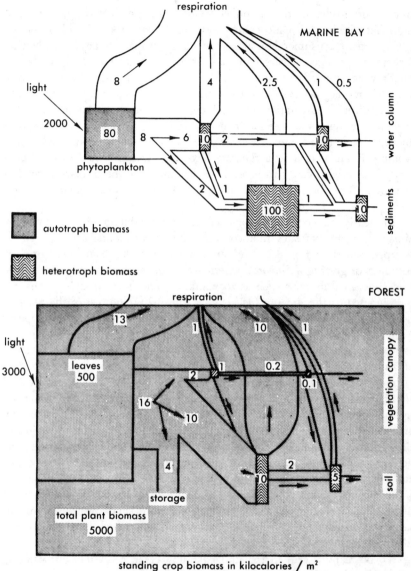

Fig. 3-2. The Y-shaped energy flow model as illustrated by a partly hypothetical diagram for a marine and a forest ecosystem. Standing crops (shaded boxes) are shown in terms of the average kcal per m² for an annual cycle and the energy flows in terms of kcal per m² per day. (Marine diagram based on the work of Riley [1956] and Harvey [1950]; forest, on the work of Ovington [1961] and Odum, Connell, and Davenport [1962].)

analysis and study. In the simplified diagram of Fig. 3-1, the bacteria and fungi that decompose plant tissues and stored plant food would be placed in the primary consumer box along with the herbivorous animals; likewise, microorganisms decomposing animal remains would go along with the secondary consumers or carnivores. However, since there is usually a considerable time lag between direct consumption of living plants and animals, and the ultimate utilization of dead organic matter, not to mention the metabolic differences between animals and microorganisms (as emphasized in Chapter 2), a much more realistic energy-flow model is obtained if the decomposers are placed in a separate box. Two working models are shown in Fig. 3-2; in each case two broad flows leading from the primary producers are shown, one for living plant tissues and one for dead organic matter.

In nearly all ecosystems some of the net production is consumed by animals or plant parasites that consume the living plants, as indicated by the upper flows in Fig. 3-2. We can conveniently designate these primary consumers as *grazing herbivores,* whether they be large animals such as cattle or deer, or small animals such as zooplankton. The flow through grazers can be designated as the *grazing food chain* (Fig. 3-2). The rest of the net production is destined to be consumed as dead organic matter of one type or another, as shown by the lower pathway in the Y-shaped diagrams of Fig. 3-2. Dead leaves, twigs, algae, etc., can be conveniently designated as plant *detritus* and the energy flow involving dead organic matter can be designated as the *detritus food chain.* As detritus is broken down, a substance called *humus* is formed, which is a complex mixture of organic matter (in various stages of decay) and heterotrophic organisms. Two types of organisms consume detritus: (1) small detritus-feeding animals, such as the soil mites or millepedes on land and various worms and mollusks in water, and (2) the bacteria and fungi of decay. These two groups are so intimately associated that it is often difficult to determine their relative effect on the breakdown of the original primary production. In many cases the two seem to be in partnership, since the reduction of large pieces to small pieces by animals makes the material more available to microorganisms, which in turn may provide food for the small animals.

To be really useful in the understanding of an ecosystem our working model must be quantitated, but unfortunately, this cannot be completely done for any known ecosystem. In Fig. 3-2, some quantities (in round numbers) are shown for two contrasting ecosystems, a shallow-water marine community and a forest. The figures are based in part on actual studies (especially in regard to standing crop and primary production) and in part on assumptions (where actual data are not available); thus the diagrams should be considered as working models to be further tested by future measurements. The marine community is characterized by a large energy flow via the grazing food chain (two thirds of P_n as shown in Fig. 3-2) and a relatively large standing crop of animals (fish, bottom fauna) as compared with plants (phytoplankton). In contrast, in the forest the major flow is via the detritus pathway (more than 90 percent of P_n), and the standing crop of plants is huge in comparison to that of animals.

Such a difference is not necessarily inherent in aquatic and terrestrial systems. In a heavily grazed pasture or grassland, 50 percent or more of the annual net production may pass down the grazing herbivore energy flow path. Since not all of the food eaten by grazers is actually assimilated, some (in feces, for example) is diverted to the decomposer route; thus the impact of the grazer on the community depends on the amount of plant material removed from the standing crop as well as on the amount of energy in the food that is utilized. Obviously, there must be a limit to direct grazing, since too rapid a removal will kill the producers or greatly reduce their future productive capacity. Range managers (applied ecologists concerned with the wise use of grasslands by man) generally work on the basis that not more than 50 percent of the forage production should be removed by cattle in a season. In natural communities there seem to be a number of feedback mechanisms that keep grazing herbivores under control, for their own good, as it were; these mechanisms will be described in a later chapter. When man takes over the control of grassland communities, he too often fails to regulate his cattle, sheep, and goats until they have gone too far.

In contrast to the grazed pasture type of ecosystem, less than 10 percent of the net production of a fertile intertidal salt marsh ecosystem is consumed by grazing herbivores, mostly insects in this case; at least 90 percent follows the detritus path of energy flow. The bulk of the animals in the marsh, such as shellfish, snails, and small crabs, seem to obtain their energy directly or indirectly from detritus. As indicated above, a similar situation usually exists in a forest. One ingenious investigator (Bray, *Oikos*, 12:70, 1961) collected autumn leaves as they fell in a deciduous forest and carefully measured "bites" taken out by the grazing insects; he came up with an estimate of 7 percent of the annual crop of leaves consumed by grazers in a season. The estimate, of course, did not include potential energy removed by sucking insects that feed on juices of the plants. Nevertheless, much of the net production in a forest clearly goes into the delayed consumer box, resulting in an abundance of consumers associated with the litter and soil. Occasionally, of course, something goes wrong and insects strip all of the leaves from trees. When this happens ecologists are often unable to determine the cause, since so little is known about the normal complex regulatory mechanisms that prevent such a "grazing cancer" in 99 out of 100 cases.

To summarize, it is convenient, even if a bit arbitrary, to divide primary consumption into two broad energy flows, and therefore to think in terms of two rather different food chains. The vegetation-rabbit-fox, or phytoplankton-zooplankton-whale, or grass-cow-man sequences are the direct, relatively simple, food chains of classical ecology. The detrital food chain is more complex, less understood, and in many ecosystems the more important. Both energy flow routes exist in nearly all ecosystems but in widely different proportions. As with any situation, extremes clearly become detrimental, but in the case of ecosystems we do not seem to know what is extreme. For example, overgrazing by definition is detrimental, but what constitutes overgrazing in different ecosystems has not been clearly defined in terms of energy flow. Likewise "undergrazing" also can be detrimental. In the complete absence of direct consumption of living plants, detritus may pile up and the release and recycling of minerals may be delayed. Microorganisms, alone, may not be able to break down the bodies of plants and release minerals fast enough if the material becomes dry or anaerobic. In terrestrial nature, fire often acts as a consumer where there is a pile-up of undecayed plant material. In some types of forest ecosystems man has learned to use fire in a controlled manner to improve the production of timber. Again, the whole ecosystem must be considered: depending on the type of ecosystem and climate, fire and grazers in moderation may be good things; in excess they are bad.

PATTERN OF WORLD DISTRIBUTION OF PRIMARY PRODUCTION

We shall close this chapter with a world-wide view of the primary productivity on which the ecosystem depends. The world distribution of primary production is shown schematically in Fig. 3-3. Values represent the average gross production rate, in grams of dry organic matter per square

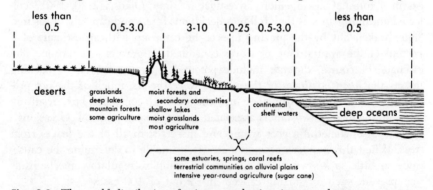

Fig. 3-3. The world distribution of primary production, in grams dry matter per square meter per day, as indicated by average daily rates of gross production in major ecosystems. Only a relatively small part of the biosphere is naturally fertile. (Redrawn from E. P. Odum, *Fundamentals of Ecology*, 2d ed. Philadelphia: Saunders, 1959.)

meter of area per day, to be expected over an annual cycle. For total annual production, multiply by 365. To visualize these values in terms of approximate kilocalories of potential food, multiply by 4. As previously indicated, as much as 90 percent of gross production may be available to heterotrophs, but it should be remembered that man or any other single species cannot assimilate all the energy fixed by plants. For example, corn stalks and wheat stubble and roots would be included in the total production of these crops but only the grain is currently consumed by man. As may be seen from Fig. 3-3, there are about three orders of magnitude in potential biological fertility of the world: (1) some parts of the open oceans and land deserts range around 0.1 gram per square meter per day or less; (2) semiarid grasslands, coastal seas, shallow lakes, and ordinary agriculture range between 1 and 10; (3) certain shallow water systems such as estuaries, coral reefs, and mineral springs together with moist forests, intensive agriculture (such as year around culture of sugar cane or cropping on irrigated deserts), and natural communities on alluvial plains may range from 10 to 20 grams per square meter per day. Production rates higher than 20 have been reported for experimental crops, polluted waters, and limited natural communities, but these values are based on short-term measurements; values higher than 25 have not been obtained for extensive areas over long periods of time.

Two tentative generalizations may be made from the data at hand. First, basic primary productivity is not necessarily a function of the kind of producer organism or the kind of medium (whether air, fresh water, or salt water), but is controlled by local supply of raw material, sun energy, and the ability of local communities as a whole (and including man) to utilize and regenerate materials for continuous reuse. Terrestrial systems are not inherently different from aquatic situations if light, water, and nutrient conditions are similar. However, large bodies of water are at a disadvantage because a large portion of light energy may be absorbed by the water before it reaches the site of maximum mineral supply. Secondly, a very large portion of the earth's surface is open ocean or arid and semiarid land and thus in the low production category, because of lack of nutrients in the former and lack of water in the latter. Many deserts can be irrigated successfully, and it is theoretically possible and perhaps feasible in the future to bring up "lost" nutrients from the bottom of the sea and thus greatly increase production. Such an "upwelling" occurs naturally in some coastal areas, and these have a productivity many times that of the average ocean. A famous example of the effect of upwelling on productivity is found along the coast of Peru. Currents are such that nutrient-rich bottom waters are constantly being brought to the surface so that phytoplankton does not suffer the usual nutrient limitations of the sea. The area supports very large populations of fish and fish-eating birds; so much guano is produced by the birds as they nest along shore that man is able to harvest it for fertilizer on a continuous-yield basis.

It now seems clear that there is a rather definite upper limit to the efficiency with which light may be utilized for the synthesis of organic matter on any large scale, and this maximum has already been achieved by some naturally adapted communities (coral reefs, for example) as well as by the most efficient agriculture. In the former, of course, production is consumed by a large variety of organisms, whereas in the latter a large portion of the net is temporarily stored and then harvested by man. Average agriculture is far below the maximum (world average grain production, for example, is only 2 grams per square meter per day). Thus, the best immediate possibilities for increasing food production for man lie in measures that reduce physical limiting factors and increase the season of growth so that sunlight is utilized for a great part of the annual cycle.

CHARTING ENERGY PATHWAYS AND MEASURING RATES OF FLOW

In the previous chapter, methods of estimating primary production were discussed in connection with the plan of study outlined for ponds and old fields. The following procedures were briefly described: dark and light bottle, diurnal curve, and chlorophyll-light methods for aquatic situations; harvest and CO_2 uptake procedures for land ecosystems. These are not the only methods, but they illustrate several basic approaches to the measurement of the rates at which light is converted into food energy by autotrophs. In the intact ecosystem it proves difficult to follow the diverging energy pathways beyond the first trophic level and to determine the exact energy source (that is, "food") used and its rate of utilization by specific populations of heterotrophs. New tools of the atomic age, such as radioactive tracers, promise to be of great service in untangling the intricate web of life that exists in even the simplest of nature. The usefulness of tracers in extending our powers of observation of function has already been mentioned, and a laboratory-type experiment was described in Chapter 2. Fig. 3-4A illustrates how tracers can be of even greater use in the field. In the photograph each individual of a single species of plant in a sample quadrat is being "labeled" by application of a solution containing radionuclides to the foliage. While some care needs to be taken in handling the concentrated solutions at the start of the experiment (hence the rubber gloves, remote control pipettes, and protective clothing), once the solution has been absorbed and dispersed in the large fluid volume of the plant biomass the concentration of radioactivity becomes so reduced that it is no longer a hazard to the investigator, nor will it have any effect on the organisms in the community

A

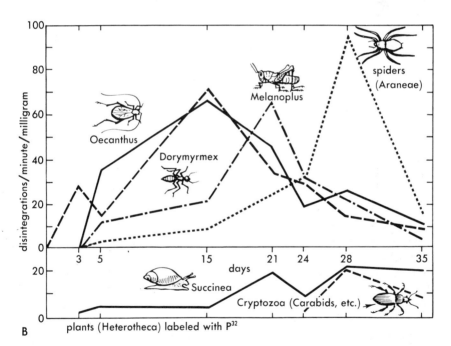

B

Fig. 3-4. A: Plants in a plot of natural grassland are being "labeled" with a radioactive tracer in order that the transfers in the food chain can be followed, as a part of a special training program in radiation ecology at the Oak Ridge Institute for Nuclear Studies. B: The results of one such experiment. The organisms most closely associated with vegetation become radioactive first, whereas considerable time is required for the tracer to reach maximum concentration in predators. (A, Oak Ridge Institute of Nuclear Studies. B, redrawn from E. P. Odum and E. J. Kuenzler, in Schultz and Klement, eds., *Radioecology*. New York: Reinhold, 1963.)

being studied. Modern instruments are so sensitive that amounts of radio-activity far less than that in a radium dial watch (which many of us wear continuously without harm) can be detected. In other words, with proper planning and precautions in setting up experiments, radioactive tracers can be as safely used out-of-doors as in the laboratory.

The results of a specific experiment carried out as shown in Fig. 3-4A are graphed in Fig. 3-4B. At intervals following the labeling of the plants with the radionuclide phosphorus-32, samples of the populations of small animals living in the grassland were collected and the amount of P^{32} in their biomass determined. Animals that became radioactive must have removed materials from the plant, or must have eaten an animal that had previously fed upon the plant. Therefore, the procedure isolates a single food chain, that is, a food chain beginning with a single kind of autotroph, in the undisturbed and intact community. As shown in Fig. 3-4B, animals that were most active in removing materials from the plant, such as the small cricket (*Oecanthus*) and the small ant (*Dorymyrmex*), reached a peak in radioactivity first. Note that radioactivity is plotted on the y axis as disintegrations per minute, which are counts per minute recorded when the samples were placed in a counter (as shown in Fig. 2-4B) corrected for radioactive decay and taking into account the efficiency of the particular instrument in recording the beta particles being emitted by the P^{32}. Larger plant

ders, such as grasshoppers (*Melanoplus*), reached a peak at a later time, wnile predators such as spiders did not reach maximum levels until about four weeks after the original labeling of the plants. There was also a delay in appearance of the P^{32} in animals such as snails and beetles that were living in the surface litter. Thus, a good separation of certain trophic and habitat niches was obtained in the experiment. Also, rate of uptake or elimination of tracers provides clues as to rates of metabolism of free-living organisms. Labeling specific energy sources or populations, and then following the fate of the labeled material has almost infinite possibilities in ecological research in the field.

In the experiment just described the tracer was used to chart the movement of materials and, indirectly, the transfer of energy through the food chain. In nature it is equally important to chart the movement of individuals as well; in such a case we would want a permanent label, one that would stay with the individual and not move from one organism to another. Fig. 3-5 illustrates one such application in which a small radioactive gold wire was inserted under the skin of a wild mouse. Radioactive gold emits penetrating gamma rays so that one may detect it at considerable distance. The mouse was a species called a golden mouse (because of its color, not because of the gold wire), which is entirely nocturnal in its activity. The day after the "tagged" mouse was released in the area from which it was trapped the investigator searched the area systematically with

Fig. 3-5. Another application of tracers. Here the objective is to trace the movement of an organism. (See text.) (Oak Ridge Institute of Nuclear Studies.)

a detector mounted on a long pole and soon located the mouse in its nest well hidden in some vines on a tree trunk, as shown in Fig. 3-5. So well was the nest hidden in this case, in fact, that the probability of finding it would have been very small without the help of the tracer. The little black box, also shown in the picture, is a device that continuously records the amount of radioactivity. By periodically reading the device, the time the mouse spent in the nest and away from it in feeding excursions can be estimated. Again we see how useful radioactive tracers can be in extending the rather limited powers of observation of a human being who cannot see in the dark, and who could not track a mouse in the tangle of vegetation in a forest even if he could see!

SUGGESTED READING LIST

CLARKE, GEORGE L., "Dynamics of production in a marine area," *Ecological Monographs*, Vol. 16 (1946), pp. 321–325.

COLE, LAMONT, "The ecosphere," *Scientific American*, April 1958, pp. 83–92.

DEEVEY, EDWARD S., "The human crop," *Scientific American*, April 1956, pp. 105–112.

GOLLEY, FRANK B., "Energy dynamics of a food chain of an old-field community," *Ecological Monographs*, Vol. 30 (1960), pp. 187–206.

LINDEMAN, RAYMOND L., "The trophic-dynamic aspect of ecology," *Ecology*, Vol. 23 (1942), pp. 399–418.

ODUM, EUGENE P., "Relationships between structure and function in the ecosystem," *Japanese Journal of Ecology*, Vol. 12 (1962), pp. 108–118.

———, 1959. *Fundamentals of ecology*, 2d ed. Philadelphia: Saunders. Chapter 3.

———, and SMALLEY, A. E., "Comparison of population energy flow of a herbivorous and a deposit-feeding invertebrate in a salt marsh ecosystem," *Proceedings of the National Academy of Science*, Vol. 45 (1959), pp. 617–622.

ODUM, HOWARD T., "Trophic structure and productivity of Silver Springs, Florida," *Ecological Monographs*, Vol. 27 (1957), pp. 55–112.

———, and PINKERTON, R. C., "Times speed regulator, the optimum efficiency for maximum output in physical and biological systems," *American Scientist*, Vol. 43 (1955), pp. 331–343.

OVINGTON, J. D., "Dry matter production by *Pinus sylvestris*," *Annals of Botany*, Vol. 4 (1957), pp. 5–58.

PEQUEGNAT, WILLIS E., "Whales, plankton and man," *Scientific American*, January 1958, pp. 84–90.

RILEY, GORDON A., "Oceanography of Long Island Sound, 1952–1954. IX Production and utilization of organic matter," *Bulletin of Bingham Oceanography College*, Vol. 15 (1956), pp. 324–344.

RYTHER, JOHN H., "Potential productivity of the sea," *Science*, Vol. 130 (1959), pp. 602–608.

TRANSEAU, E. N., "The accumulation of energy by plants," *Ohio Journal of Science*, Vol. 26 (1926), pp. 1–10.

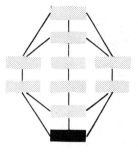

CHAPTER FOUR

BIOGEOCHEMICAL

CYCLES In the preceding chapter important principles and some

orders of magnitude regarding energy flow in ecosystems were discussed. As already emphasized, the movement of materials in the ecosystem is an equally important consideration. The more or less circular paths of the chemical elements passing back and forth between organisms and environment are known as *biogeochemical cycles*. "Bio" refers to living organisms and "geo" to the rocks, soil, air, and water of the earth. Geochemistry is an important physical science, concerned with the chemical composition of the earth and the exchange of elements between different parts of the earth's crust and its oceans, rivers, etc. Biogeochemistry is thus the study of the exchange (that is, back and forth movement) of materials between living and nonliving components of the biosphere.

In Fig. 4-1 a biogeochemical cycle is superimposed on a simplified energy-flow diagram to show the interrelation of the two basic processes. Vital elements in nature are never, or almost never, homogeneously distributed nor present in the same chemical form throughout an ecosystem. Rather, materials exist in compartments, or *pools*, with varying rates of exchange between them. From the ecological standpoint it is advantageous to distinguish between a large, slow-moving nonbiological pool and a smaller but more active pool that is exchanging rapidly with organisms. In Fig. 4-1 the large reservoir is the box labeled "pool" and the rapidly cycling material is represented by the stippled circle going from autotrophs to heterotrophs and back again. Sometimes the reservoir portion is called the unavailable pool and the cycling portion the available pool; such a designation is permissible provided it is clearly understood that the terms are relative. An atom in the reservoir pool is not necessarily permanently unavailable to organisms but only relatively so; in comparison, an atom in the cycling pool is instantly available. Almost always there is a slow movement of atoms between the unavailable and the available pools.

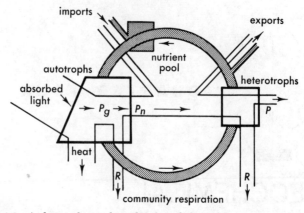

Fig. 4-1. A biogeochemical cycle (stippled circle) superimposed upon a simplified energy-flow diagram, contrasting the cycling of material with the one-way flow of energy. P_g = gross production; P_n = net primary production, which may be consumed within the system by heterotrophs or stored or exported from the system.

AMOUNTS VERSUS RATES

When a farmer sends a sample of soil to the soils laboratory of his state university for routine testing, the sample is often treated with 0.1 normal acid or alkali solution. The quantity of minerals, such as phosphorus, calcium, or potassium, removed by such gentle treatments is considered a crude measure of quantities available to plants (that is, the size of the available pools). Long experience in agriculture has shown that a simple test such as this may provide a useful basis for fertilizer recommendations, but as often as not leaves much to be desired. As with energy, it is evident that the rates of movement or cycling may be more important in determining biological productivity than the amount present in any one place at any one time. Radioactive isotopes have been a great help in determining rates of movements since tagged atoms can actually be followed as they exchange with organism and environment. These new tools of the atomic age have revealed unknown transfers and unexpected rapid rates of exchange in many instances, and thus are helping to produce major breakthroughs in our knowledge of biogeochemical cycles. No ecologist of the coming generation can afford to overlook these new tools in his study of such complex ecosystems as oceans, lakes, and forests.

NUTRIENTS

Elements and dissolved salts essential to life may be conveniently termed *biogenic salts* or *nutrients* and divided into two groups, the *macronutrients* and the *micronutrients*. The former include elements and their compounds that have key roles in protoplasm and that are needed in relatively large quantities, as for example, carbon, hydrogen, oxygen, nitrogen, potassium, calcium, magnesium, sulfur, and phosphorus. The micronutrients include those elements and their compounds also necessary for the operation of living systems but required only in very minute quantities. At least ten micronutrients are known to be required for primary production: iron, manganese, copper, zinc, boron, sodium, molybdenum, chlorine, vanadium, and cobalt. Several of these—for example, sodium—may rate as macronutrients for certain heterotrophs that may also require additional elements such as iodine. No list should be considered complete, for a number of elements are on the suspect list and may have biological importance. Since micronutrients may occur in an environment in even more minute quantity than required by an organism, their lack may limit productivity to the same degree as a shortage of a macronutrient.

It should be emphasized at this point that many elements that have no known biological function also circulate between organisms and environment. Nonessential elements may be of great ecological importance if they occur in quantities that are chemically toxic, if they react to bind or make unavailable essential elements, or, especially, if they are radioactive (for example, strontium-90). We shall have much to say about the latter subsequently. Thus, the ecologist is concerned with nearly all of the natural elements of the periodic table as well as with the newer man-made ones, such as plutonium.

The Sulfur Cycle in Aquatic Environments

The sulfur cycle as diagramed in Fig. 4-2 illustrates the main features of a biogeochemical cycle in a specific ecosystem. The cycling and reservoir pools, the chemical forms of the elements, and the organisms involved are all shown in the diagram. Sulfate (SO_4) in the water is the principal available form that is reduced by autotrophic plants and incorporated into proteins, sulfur being an essential constituent of certain amino acids. When the bodies of plants and animals are decomposed by heterotrophic microorganisms, hydrogen sulfide (H_2S) is released. Some of the H_2S is then reconverted to sulfate by specialized sulfur bacteria. Some of these bacteria are called chemosynthetic organisms, because they obtain their own energy from the chemical oxidation of inorganic compounds (in this case oxidation of sulfide to sulfur, etc.) instead of from light as do photosynthetic organisms. Since the major site of decomposition is in the sediments, anaerobic conditions tend to develop, with the result that much of the H_2S may not be oxidized but may pass into the reservoir pool as shown in Fig. 4-2. Interestingly, when iron compounds are formed, phosphorus is converted from insoluble to soluble form and thus becomes available to living organ-

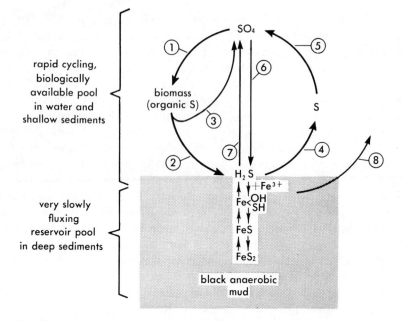

Fig. 4-2. The sulfur cycle as an illustration of the movement of a specific element in a specific ecosystem. Organisms play key roles in the rapidly cycling pool as follows: (1) primary production by autotrophs; (2) decomposition by heterotrophic microorganisms; (3) animal excretion; (4), (5) steps by specialized colorless, purple and green sulfur bacteria; (6) desulfovibrio bacteria (anaerobic sulfate reducers); (7) thiobacilli bacteria (aerobic sulfide oxidizers). Step 8 releases phosphorus (from insoluble ferric phosphate), thus speeding up the cycling of this vital element.

isms in the water. Here is an excellent illustration of how one nutrient cycle regulates another.

That organisms, especially microorganisms, play key roles is true not only in the sulfur cycle but in the nitrogen cycle and most of the others. Organisms are not just passive actors in a physical and chemical milieu, but are active participants in the regulation of their own environment. No one organism or population alone has much control, of course, but the sum total of processes in the well-ordered ecosystem insures continuous supplies of materials and energy needed for life. Redfield (1958), for example, has marshalled the evidence to indicate that organisms over long periods of time have largely controlled the chemical composition of the sea. Since man, equipped with bulldozers and other powerful machinery, is becoming a powerful geochemical agent, he needs to take long, hard looks at well-ordered ecosystems. As a dependent heterotroph he cannot alone control the biosphere for his own good; he must have the cooperation of the "germs" of the soil and water as well as the autotrophs and many other organisms. Too often, man works to obtain a temporary advantage by increasing the rate of flow of materials, but forgets to arrange for the return mechanism. The frequent failure of tropical agriculture is a good example. Often a few years of good crops are followed by declining productivity as the nutrients leach away or otherwise become unavailable. The failure lies in the fact that the biological return mechanisms that existed in the original system have not been engineered into the man-ordered system.

Now is as good a time as any to point out that the area of microbial ecology is one of the more important areas of ecology, and, at present, one of the least known. We can draw in the over-all aspects of the sulfur cycle in broad brush strokes but the details are unknown. Until numbers can be obtained for the flux rates indicated by the arrows, we have essentially nothing that can be used in any practical manner. It is not easy to leave the security of the laboratory and go out into the field, but it is important that more well-trained microbiologists tackle the microbial populations as they actually operate in nature. New tools developed in the laboratory now make it possible to work in nature also.

THE TWO BASIC TYPES OF BIOGEOCHEMICAL CYCLES

From the standpoint of the biosphere as a whole, biogeochemical cycles fall into two groups: the sedimentary type as illustrated by the sulfur cycle and the gaseous type as illustrated by the nitrogen cycle, shown in Fig. 4-3. In the latter the air is the great reservoir and safety valve of the system. Nitrogen is continually feeding into and out of this great reservoir from the rapidly cycling pool associated with organisms. Both biological and nonbiological mechanisms are involved in denitrification and nitrogen fixing, the latter being the conversion of the nitrogen of the air, which is not available to autotrophs, to nitrates, which are. As in the case of the sulfur cycle, specialized microorganisms play key roles. For example, only a relatively few species of bacteria and blue-green algae, which, fortunately, are very abundant in many systems, can fix nitrogen. No so-called higher plant or animal has this ability. Legumes fix nitrogen only through the specialized bacteria that live in their roots. The self-regulating feedback mechanisms, as shown in a very simplified manner in Fig. 4-3, make the nitrogen and other gaseous-type cycles (such as the carbon or water cycles) relatively perfect in terms of large areas of the biosphere. Any increase in movement along one path is quickly compensated for by adjustments along other paths. Locally, however, nitrogen often becomes limiting to the biological system either because regeneration (that is, movement from unavailable to available) is too slow or a net loss is occurring from the local system.

Most nutrients are more earthbound than nitrogen; their cycles are

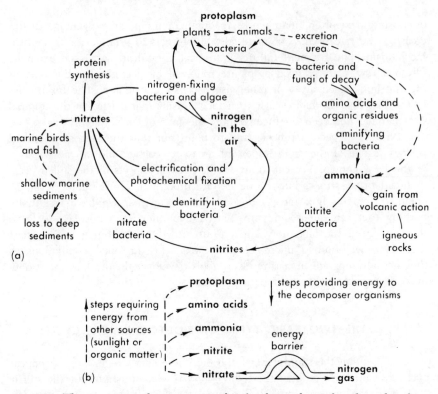

Fig. 4-3. The nitrogen cycle as an example of a biogeochemical cycle with a large gaseous reservoir and many feedback mechanisms. (Redrawn from E. P. Odum, *Fundamentals of Ecology*, 2d ed. Philadelphia: Saunders, 1959.)

less perfect and, consequently, more easily disrupted by man. The phosphorus cycle is a good example of a sedimentary cycle of the utmost importance. Phosphorus is required for nearly all the basic energy transformations that distinguish living protoplasm from nonliving systems, and it is relatively rare on the earth's surface in terms of biological demand. Organisms have evolved many hoarding devices for this element; hence the concentration of phosphorus in a gram of biomass is usually many times that in a gram of surrounding environment (water, for example). The beautiful and efficient way in which the ATP system works within the cell to conserve both energy and materials is described in *Cell Structure and Function,* in this series. As the cycling pool of phosphorus spins around in the organism and in local biogeochemical cycles there is nevertheless a tendency for a slow downhill movement of the reservoir phosphorus, following the pattern of erosion and sedimentation. In the long range, return or replacement occurs as a result of both physical and biological processes. Weathering of rocks, airborne dust, volcanic gases (that is, natural fall-out), and bits of salt spray picked up by the wind are routes that may move small amounts of material uphill. Upwelling of deep ocean waters bringing phosphorus from the unlighted depths to the photosynthetic zone is a very important return mechanism in the sea. The fish-eating guano birds, mentioned in Chapter 3, that annually excrete many tons of phosphorus on their nesting grounds on the west coast of South America are examples of agents in biological recycling. Hutchinson (1948) has shown that return of phosphorus from the sea to land as the result of fish harvested by birds and man is of no small magnitude. In well-ordered systems such as a coral reef (see also Chapter 1) one is impressed with the numerous biological mechanisms that keep the net loss of materials to a very minimum amount, perhaps no more than is returned by natural means. In many areas, however, man has so increased the rate of erosion that the one-way movement of phosphorus into the large unavailable pool in the deep ocean sediments has been increased. Hutchinson estimates that at the present time natural means of return are inadequate to keep up with the downhill loss. For the present, agricultural man is not particularly worried, since he is able to mine the considerable reserves of phosphate rock and replace some of the loss. Someday, however, it may be necessary to improve the retention within man-ordered systems and to return materials from the deep sea; it is probable that atomic energy will be used for the latter purpose.

Regardless of whether we are dealing with biological units or inorganic chemicals, both the standing state and the rates of change in the standing state are of vital importance. Most especially, we must be concerned with the relationship between the amounts, the structure (that is, how arranged in space), and the rates. Only by obtaining maximum information in all these areas can we hope to understand and thereby manage nature.

NUTRIENT CYCLING AND ENERGY FLOW AT THE POPULATION LEVEL

The emphasis thus far has been on the over-all situation in large ecosystems. An example of a study at the population level is the work of Kuenzler (1961), who has measured both energy flow and the cycling of phosphorus in a population of shellfish living in a salt-marsh ecosystem. The ribbed mussel, *Modiolus demissus*, is one of the abundant animals living in salt marshes that form a belt between the outer barrier islands and the mainland along the coast of the southeastern United States. The mussel, which is about the size of an oyster, lives in small colonies attached to the substrate throughout the marsh. On the basis of random samples, Kuenzler found that the numbers varied from about 8 per square meter average to 32 per square meter in the more favorable spots. Organic biomass (ash-free dry weight) averaged 12 grams per square meter, which is approximately equivalent to 60 large or kilogram Calories (that is, 60 kcal per m^2).

Measurements of growth and respiration indicated that the population energy flow was a modest 56 kcal per square meter per year. However, in obtaining its food of small organisms and particles from the sea water that covers the marsh with each tide, the mussels filter very large quantities of water. As a result, a large amount of particulate matter or detritus is removed from the water and sedimented on the surface of the marsh. The particles, which are rich in phosphorus, other minerals, and vitamins, are thus retained in the marsh by action of the mussel instead of being carried out by the tide. Kuenzler was able to calculate that the turnover time of particulate phosphorus in the water due to the action of the mussel population was only 2.6 days. That is, the mussels removed from the water every two and one-half days a quantity of phosphorus equal to the average amount present in the particles in the water (estimated to equal about 14 milligrams per square meter). The population was also found to have marked, although less, effect on cycling of dissolved phosphorus (estimated to equal about 25 milligrams per square meter). The study is summarized in Fig. 4-4, which shows amounts and flux rates.

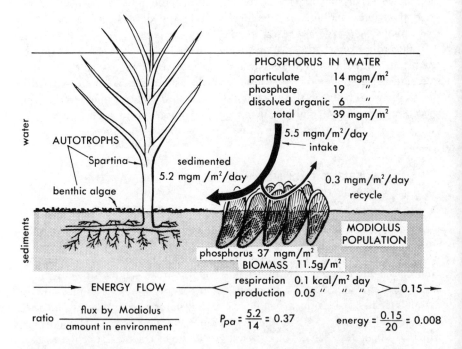

Fig. 4-4. The role of a shellfish (mussel) population in the cycling and retention of phosphorus in an estuarine ecosystem. The population has a major effect on the distribution of phosphorus even though the species is but a small component in the community in terms of biomass and energy flow. (Based on data from E. J. Kuenzler, *Limnology and Oceanography*, Vol. 6, 1961.)

Although the mussels are a relatively minor component of the marsh in terms of biomass and energy flow, they proved to have a major effect on the cycling and retention of valuable phosphorus. The mussel is not particularly important as a direct source of food for man or other animals, since the production (or growth) per year is not great in comparison with production of other populations, but the species is important as an agent helping to maintain fertility and, thereby, production of autotrophs. To put it another way, Kuenzler's study demonstrated that the mussel population is more important to the ecosystem as a biogeochemical agent than as a transformer of energy. Here again is an excellent illustration of the point previously made: species in nature may have great value to man in an indirect way not apparent on superficial examination. A species does not have to be a link in man's food chain to be valuable. Man needs the help of many species in maintaining stability and fertility of his environment.

FALL-OUT AND STRONTIUM-90

In addition to bringing about some large-scale changes in the rate of movement of the basic elements of the biosphere, man has recently begun adding some entirely new radioactive materials to biogeochemical cycles. The long-term biological effects of these new additions are matters of considerable controversy, which, as always, means that both our knowledge and our ability to interpret what data we do have are inadequate. Complex questions of pathology (cancer, etc.), genetics (mutations, etc.), and ecology are involved. The environmental fate of the man-made radioactive substances and their movement in food chains are aspects of particular interest to the ecologist as well as to the general public.

When uranium atoms split or "fission" in the chain reactions of nuclear reactors or nuclear weapons tests, a group of radioactive nuclides called *fission products* are produced; they are pieces of the uranium atom left over after part of the mass of the uranium atom has been converted into energy. Most fission products involve elements such as strontium or cesium that are not essential for life; nevertheless they get into food chains and become incorporated into biomass, and because they are radioactive they can have biological effects even if present only in very small amounts. Another class of radioactive isotopes, the *nonfission products,* may also be produced in weapons or reactors when neutrons (nuclear particles with no electrical charge) activate materials that happen to be in the path of the high-energy particles. Radioisotopes of biologically important elements such as carbon, zinc, and iron can be formed in this manner. This, of course, is one of the ways isotopes are produced for research purposes. Fission and nonfission products alike are injected into the atmosphere by small nuclear weapons and into the stratosphere by large weapons; eventually they come down to earth again in what we call atomic fall-out along with rain, dust, and other natural "fall-out." While much of the radioactive debris from small weapons may come down within a few hundred miles, the fall-out from large hydrogen bomb weapons is almost worldwide. Because essentially the same radio-active materials become waste products of power reactors and other peaceful uses of atomic energy, environmental fate and effect of the radioactive by-products are still matters of great concern to mankind even if no more nuclear weapons were to be exploded.

As pointed out in the discussion of a tracer experiment in Chapter 2, organisms tend to "hoard" nutrients, so that concentrations within biomass often greatly exceed the concentration in the immediate physical environment. Therefore, radioisotopes of nutrients, being chemically identical to the stable isotopes, will also be concentrated, often creating local radiation fields in cells and tissues more intense than in the surrounding environment. For example, small amounts of radioactive phosphorus released into the Columbia river by reactors located on shore were found to become concentrated in the eggs of wild geese that obtained their food from the river. The amount of radiophosphorus in a gram of the yolk of the eggs proved to be several thousand times that present in a gram of river water.

Of all the man-made radioactive materials, the fission product strontium-90 seems to be of the greatest immediate concern to man for the following reasons: (1) it is a common component of atomic fall-out, as well as of atomic wastes, throughout the world; (2) it loses its radioactivity very slowly (in technical terms it has a half-life of 28 years) in contrast to many fission products that decay to harmless levels in a few hours or days; (3) strontium behaves chemically like calcium, an abundant and biologically important element, and strontium-90 therefore follows natural (nonradioactive) strontium and calcium into biogeochemical cycles; (4) it is taken up by plants more readily than most fall-out materials, both directly by foliage absorption and via soil and water; (5) when taken in with food by man and vertebrates it becomes concentrated and retained by bone in close proximity to blood-making tissue in bone marrow, which is especially sensitive to radiation damage.

Dr. J. L. Kulp of the Lamont Geochemical Laboratories (see Suggested Readings at the end of this chapter) estimates that by 1960 about 4 million curies of strontium-90 were in the biosphere, with about 50 millicuries per square mile of land surface in the Northern Hemisphere and about 15 millicuries per square mile in southern latitudes. A curie is an amount of radioactive substance emitting about two trillion radiations per minute (technically, 2.2×10^{12} atoms disintegrating per minute); a millicurie is $\frac{1}{1000}$ or 10^{-3} curies. Most of this, of course, remains in the general nonbiological mineral pool, but small amounts are now moving in biological cycles. In 1959 it was estimated that bones of children in North American and Europe averaged 2.6, and bones of adults 0.4, micromicrocuries of strontium-90 per gram of bone calcium. A micromicrocurie equals 10^{-12} curies, or an amount emitting 2.2 radiations per minute. While the average amount in human tissue is thus still very tiny and not thought to be harmful, it has been increasing steadily since the beginning of nuclear weapons testing in the 1940s.

Ecologically speaking, strontium-90 from fall-out (and also potentially from waste disposal) gets into man and animals especially readily through the grazing food chain in ecosystems having high rainfall, low calcium and mineral concentrations (that is, low fertility), and heavy grazing (that is, rapid consumption and small standing crop of vegetation). (Think about this a moment and see if you can figure out why each of these conditions might favor entrance of fall-out into biological systems.) In England it has been found that the bones of sheep that graze on moors, which have acid soils and high rainfalls, contained many times more strontium-90 than the bones of sheep grazing in more fertile, drier lowland pastures. Likewise, especially high concentrations have been found in the bone and flesh of reindeer and caribou on arctic tundras where the mattlike vegetation of sedges, lichens, and grasses, on which the animals feed, acts as an especially efficient fall-out trap. A grass-cow-milk route, of course, is one way in which man gets strontium-90 into his bones. Not drinking milk may not help because vegetables, fruit, or almost any food one might choose also may be contaminated.

While most investigators who are studying the problem believe that man-made radioactivity so far introduced into the biosphere does not present a hazard to the human population, no one wants to see the concentrations increased any more than is necessary from the standpoint of security and the useful exploitation of atomic energy. The sheep and reindeer situation warn what could happen if population pressure forced man to shorten his food chain and rely more heavily on direct consumption of field crops. There is one good side to all this: in the past 15 years we have learned a great deal about the biogeochemistry of our biosphere as a result of the many tracers inadvertently injected into the system. We could learn enough from these vast experiments to keep us out of trouble in the future. In fact, the special care that man must now observe with radioactive contamination may be the means of reducing other environmental contamination such as water pollution, smog, and insecticides that are at the present time actually a greater health hazard than fall-out. In other words, since all environmental pollution problems are interrelated, keeping close watch on one aspect should help control other aspects. The study of the ecology of atomic waste disposal areas at the Oak Ridge National Laboratory and elsewhere is now being accelerated in the belief that such experimental areas provide a key to our understanding not only of specific atomic energy waste problems but of other pollution problems as well.

SUGGESTED READING LIST

COLE, LaMONT C., "The ecosphere," *Scientific American*, April 1958, pp. 83–92.

HUTCHINSON, G. EVELYN, "Nitrogen in the biogeochemistry of the atmosphere," *American Scientist*, Vol. 32 (1944), pp. 178–195.

——, "On living in the biosphere," *Scientific Monthly*, Vol. 67 (1948), pp. 393–398.

KAMEN, MARTIN D., "Discoveries in nitrogen fixation," *Scientific American*, March 1953, pp. 38–43.

KUENZLER, EDWARD J., "Phosphorus budget of a mussel population," *Limnology and Oceanography*, Vol. 6 (1961), pp. 400–415.

KULP, J. L., "Radionuclides in man from nuclear tests," *Journal of Agriculture and Food Chemistry*, Vol. 9 (1961), pp. 122–126.

——, SLAKTER, R., and SCHULERT, A. R., "Strontium-90 in food," *Journal of Agriculture and Food Chemistry*, Vol. 7 (1959), pp. 466–469. See also articles in *Science* (Vol. 132; pp. 448–454) and 3-volume technical summary (published by LaMont Geochemical Laboratory, Columbia Univ.) by Kulp and co-workers.

ODUM, EUGENE P., 1959. *Fundamentals of ecology*, 2d ed. Philadelphia: Saunders. Chapter 3, pages 30–42; Chapter 14.

REDFIELD, ALFRED C., "The biological control of chemical factors in the environment," *American Scientist*, Vol. 46 (1958), pp. 205–221.

VALLENTYNE, JOHN R., 1960. "Biosphere, geochemistry of," *McGraw-Hill encyclopedia of science and technology*, Vol. 2, pp. 239–245.

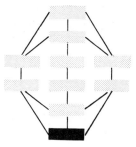

CHAPTER FIVE

LIMITING

FACTORS—

LIEBIG'S LAW

EXTENDED
In the previous chapters we have seen how the flow of energy and the cycling of materials limit and regulate the biological community, and how the community in turn regulates, within some limits at least, the flux rates. In addition, we have hinted that two other important aspects need to be considered, namely: (1) environmental factors, such as temperature, that are not directly involved in biological energy or material transformations, but that determine the "condition of existence" for living organisms; (2) the interactions of organisms with organisms, which in many communities have profound effects on the size and composition of populations. Since all four of these aspects—*energy, materials, conditions, and community*—interact in complex ways in nature, it would be well to consider the general principles of *limiting factors* before we move on to the discussion of the more purely biological factors in ecosystems.

Any factor that tends to slow down potential growth in an ecosystem is said to be a limiting factor. Where the brake, as it were, has survival value, as in the case of the herbivore limitation discussed in Chapter 3, the term *regulatory factor* may be more appropriate. The idea that organisms may be controlled by the weakest link in the ecological chain of requirements goes back at least to the time of Justus Liebig (1840), who was a pioneer in the study of inorganic chemical fertilizers in agriculture.

Liebig was impressed with the fact that crop plants were often limited by whatever essential element was in short supply, regardless of whether the total amount required was large or small. Liebig's "law of the minimum" has come to mean that the rate of growth is dependent on the nutrient or

65

other conditions present in the minimum quantity in terms of need and availability. If we extend this idea to include the limiting effect of the maximum (that is, too much can also limit) and recognize that factors interact (that is, short supply of one thing affects requirements for another thing not in itself limiting), we end up with a working principle that is very useful in the study of any specific ecosystem or any part thereof.

We may restate the extended concept of limiting factors as follows: the success of a population or community depends on a complex of conditions; any condition that approaches or exceeds the limit of tolerance for the organism or group in question may be said to be a limiting factor. Although the incoming energy of the sun and the laws of thermodynamics set the ultimate limits in all of the biosphere, different ecosystems have different combinations of factors that may put further limitations on biological structure and function.

The chief value of the limiting factor concept lies in the fact that it gives the ecologist an "entering wedge" into the study of complicated situations. Environmental relations are indeed complex, so it is fortunate that not all factors are of equal ecological importance. Oxygen, for example, is a physiological necessity to all animals, but it becomes a limiting factor from the ecological standpoint only in certain environments. If fish are dying in a polluted stream, for example, oxygen concentration in the water would be one of the first things we would investigate, since oxygen in water is variable, easily depleted, and often is in short supply. If small mammals are dying in a field, however, we would look for some other cause, since oxygen in the air is constant and abundant in terms of need by the population (that is, not easily depleted by biological activity), and, therefore, not likely to be limiting.

THE EXPERIMENTAL APPROACH TO STUDY OF LIMITING FACTORS

The prefix "eury" is often used to indicate wide limits of tolerance and "steno" to indicate narrow limits. Among fish, trout are in general more stenothermal than bass in that they are not able to tolerate as wide a range of temperatures. If we cut down all the trees along a mountain stream, allowing the sun to warm up the water a few degrees, the trout might be killed and the bass persist. Organisms with wide limits of tolerance, of course, are likely to be widely distributed, but wide limits for one factor does not necessarily mean wide limits for all factors. A plant might be eurythermal but stenohydric (have narrow limits of tolerance for water); or an animal such as a trout might be stenothermal but euryphagic (feed on a wide variety of food).

Limits of physiological tolerance for such things as temperature or nutrients can often be determined with precision in the laboratory, but one should be cautious about transferring such knowledge to the field. As we have previously pointed out, what is true at the organism level may be only part of the story at the community level. Quite frequently organisms do not actually live in nature under optimum conditions for a specific factor. As a good example we may cite the work of Kinne (1956), who found that a particular species of shallow-water marine coelenterate would grow under a wide range of salinity but attained the best growth at a salinity of 16 parts of salt per thousand parts of water. The organism was not found at this optimum in nature, however, but was found living at lower salinities. Obviously, something was more important in nature than salinity. One would need to analyze the field situation and then return to the laboratory for experiments with other factors or combinations of factors. The search for limiting factors is much like detective work and can be equally absorbing.

The open sea provides another example of the experimental approach to the study of limiting factors. In recent years a great deal of progress has been made in the study of primary production in the ocean. Such work is motivated by the scientist's curiosity about the tiny plants that are so different in size and morphology from land plants, and also by the realization that man may someday have to farm the sea. In the photic (lighted) zone of the open sea, most nutrients are relatively scarce and therefore are limiting factor suspects. However, when so many nutrients are in low concentration, the chemical observations normally made at sea do not provide any information as to which nutrient is actually limiting the production at a particular time or place. Investigators from the Woods Hole Oceanographic Institution have found that simple enrichment experiments set up on board a research vessel help answer the question. The experiments entail adding various nutrients one by one to water containing the natural phytoplankton. The rate of uptake of radioactive carbon (C^{14}), while the water samples are held for 24 hours under constant illumination in containers aboard the ship, is used as an index of the net carbon fixation in photosynthesis. (Recall dark and light bottle experiments mentioned in Chapter 2.) When nitrogen or phosphorus was added to the water from the Sargasso Sea, which is one of the more or less desert areas of the ocean mentioned in Chapter 3, no increase in C^{14} uptake occurred (as compared with control samples not enriched), even though these nutrients are so commonly limiting in the sea. When either silica or iron was added, however, carbon uptake immediately increased, thus indicating that the micronutrients were either directly limiting or in some way necessary for full use of the macronutrients. In other words, adding a lot of nitrate and phosphate fertilizer in the area would not increase food production unless the silicate and iron limitations were first overcome by enrichment with these nutrients.

Factor Compensation

Caution is necessary not only in transferring laboratory data on tolerances to the field but in transferring such data from one region to another, even when the same species are involved. Species with wide geographical ranges often develop locally adapted populations, called *ecotypes*, having different limits of tolerance to temperature, light, or other factors. Compensation along a gradient of conditions may involve genetic races (with or without morphological manifestations) or merely acclimatization. Reciprocal transplants often reveal whether ecotypes are actually genetic races. The possibility of genetic fixation in local strains has often been overlooked in applied ecology, with the result that restocking or transplanting has often failed because individuals from remote regions were used.

A good example of temperature compensation within the species is shown in Fig. 5-1A. Small jellyfish move through the water by rhythmical contractions that expel water from the central cavity in a sort of jet propulsion. A pulsation rate of about 15 to 20 per minute seems to be optimum. Note that individuals living in the northern sea at Halifax swim at approximately the same rate as individuals in southern seas, even though the water temperature may be 20° C lower.

Fig. 5-1B illustrates partial light compensation by plant populations. Alpine grasslands at low latitudes and in the arctic may be subject to similar

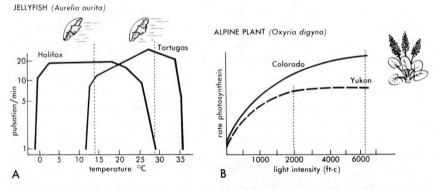

Fig. 5-1. Physical factor compensation by animals and plants. A: How different populations of the same species (i.e., ecotypes) of jellyfish are adapted to swim at temperatures of their environment. The dotted vertical lines represent the average water temperature in summer at the northern (Halifax) and southern (Tortugas) locations. B: How populations of an alpine plant in the Yukon, where light intensity is low, reach maximum photosynthetic rate at a lower light intensity (about 2000 foot candles, as indicated by the first dotted line) than plants in high mountains of Colorado where light intensity is high. (*Left*, redrawn from T. H. Bullock, *Biological Reviews*, Vol. 30, 1955, after Mayer. *Right*, redrawn from H. A. Mooney and W. D. Billings, *Ecological Monographs*, Vol. 31, 1961.)

low temperatures but to very different light intensities. As shown in the diagram, the plants in the Yukon Territory reach their peak of photosynthesis (that is, light saturation) at a lower light intensity than the more southern alpine populations in Colorado, in harmony with the generally lower intensity in the former region.

Although many species are able to compensate along an extensive gradient, such as a north-south temperature gradient, more complete adaptation is often accomplished from the ecological standpoint by a series of closely related species that replace one another along the gradient. For example, along the seashore in New England small white snails, or periwinkles, are abundant in the intertidal zone; *Littorina littorea* is usually the most common species. Further south, along the South Atlantic coast, this species is replaced in the same intertidal zone by a very similar but distinct species, *Littorina irrorata*. We have already remarked on the importance of such ecological equivalence in Chapter 3. In many ways interspecific compensation of this sort is more efficient than intraspecific compensation since a wider range of genetic material is available.

ECOLOGICAL INDICATORS

Despite the wide range of adaptation, certain species may sometimes serve as useful indicators of environmental conditions. From what we have just said it is obvious that "steno" species make more reliable indicators than "eury" species. Therefore, the rarer species often make the best indicators. Range managers, for example, find that the decline of certain relatively rare species of plants that are sensitive to grazing will indicate the approach of overgrazing before it becomes apparent in the grassland as a whole. A group of species or the whole community, of course, provides the best indicator of conditions, although harder to assess. Investigators studying stream pollution have found that a decline in the number of species or in a diversity index (as discussed in Chapter 2) often indicates pollution before the total number of individuals or the total productivity are measurably affected. Employing the species structure or the diversity ratio as a sensitive index may enable the applied worker to recognize and correct a situation involving a limiting factor before it becomes critical.

To summarize, there are three important points regarding limiting factors to be kept constantly in mind: (1) Coordinated field observation, field experimentation, and laboratory experimentation are almost always necessary in the investigation of limiting factors at the ecological level. (2) The presence of a species in two different regions does not necessarily mean that the environmental conditions are the same in the two regions; although rare species or "steno" species sometimes make good indicators, groups of species or the community as a whole is more reliable. (3) Communities are able to adapt or compensate so that the over-all rates of function, such as energy flow and productivity, may remain the same over a considerable part of a gradient of conditions even though the species structure may change drastically. Thus, within the middle range of temperatures in the biosphere, northern communities may be able to fix and transfer as much energy as southern communities on a yearly average (assuming, of course, that conditions other than temperature are not too extreme). Within fairly wide limits, therefore, differences in conditions of existence have more effect at the species level than at the ecosystem level. When the conditions do approach the extremes of a gradient, the number of species declines first, followed by decline in the *rates of function* as the conditions become limiting for any and all life (as in deserts or in the arctic). As pointed out in Chapter 2, stability also is affected in that the standing crop and the rate of function fluctuate or oscillate more violently than is the case under the moderate range of conditions of existence.

CONDITIONS OF EXISTENCE AS REGULATORY FACTORS

Light, temperature, and water (rainfall) are ecologically important environmental factors on land; light, temperature, and salinity are the big three in the sea. In fresh water, other factors, such as oxygen, may be of major importance. All of these conditions of existence may not only be limiting factors in the detrimental sense but also regulatory factors in the beneficial sense that adapted organisms respond to these factors in such a way that the community achieves the maximum homeostasis possible under the conditions. Discussion of the many mechanisms by which organisms adapt is beyond the scope of this volume; an example or two will serve to illustrate the extensive role of physical factors in coordinating biological activity.

No physical factor is of greater interest to the ecologist than light. It is, first, the ultimate source of energy for all life; second, a limiting factor (since too little or too much kills); and, third, an extremely important regulator of daily and seasonal activities for a great many organisms, both plant and animal. Three aspects of light are of great interest: (1) the intensity, as illustrated in Fig. 5-1B, (2) the wavelength, and (3) the duration. As shown in Fig. 5-2, visible light is but a small part of an extensive radiation spectrum of electromagnetic energy ranging from very short to very long wavelengths. Infrared, ultraviolet, and x rays also have ecological importance, but our attention here will be on the visible rays. One of the most dependable environmental cues by which organisms time their activities in temperate zones is the day-length period, or photoperiod (Fig. 5-3). In contrast to

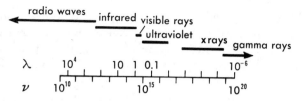

Fig. 5-2. The spectrum of electromagnetic radiations. $\lambda =$ wavelength in microns; $\nu =$ frequency in seconds.

temperature, photoperiod is always the same for a given season and locality, year after year. Photoperiod has been shown to be the timer or trigger that sets off a physiological sequence that brings about molting, fat deposition, migration, and breeding in temperate-zone birds. Not all of the details have been worked out, but our present understanding of photoperiod regulation of the annual cycle in birds is shown in Fig. 5-4. On the wintering ground in autumn and early winter, the bird is refractory to photoperiod stimulus; that is, the internal mechanism will not respond to a day-length

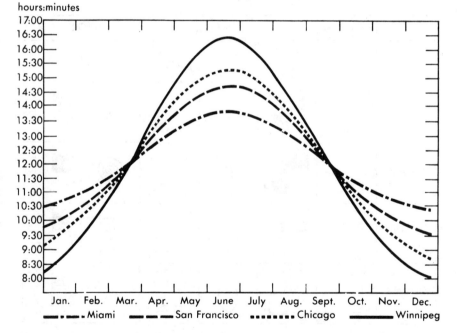

Fig. 5-3. Variations in length of day or photoperiod at four latitudes in North America. Photoperiod is an important regulator of seasonal activity in both plants and animals, especially in north temperate regions where seasonal changes in day length are pronounced. The cocklebur requires a short day (15 hours or less) and hence does not flower at Winnipeg until the days begin to shorten in late summer. At Miami, however, the days are always short enough so that the plant flowers whenever physiologically ripe. (Redrawn from F. B. Salisbury, *Scientific American*, May 1952.)

stimulus. Short days of fall are apparently necessary to reset and rewind the biological clock, as it were. Any time after December the bird will respond to an increase in day length. In nature, of course, stimulation does not occur until the approach of the long days of late winter or spring. However, one can produce out-of-season fat deposition, migratory restlessness, and an increase in size of reproductive organs in mid-winter in the laboratory by an artificial increase in the light period. Interestingly enough, the intensity of the extra light is not a factor so long as the light is stronger than full moonlight; thus the adaptation neatly avoids false stimulation by moonlight on the one hand, and the effects of varying daylight intensity due to cloud cover on the other hand.

As shown in Fig. 5-4, photoperiod is believed to act through the hypothalamic part of the brain (by way of the eye), which produces a neurohormone that stimulates the pituitary gland (the master endocrine gland), which in turn sends out the several different hormones in sequence to the target organs. The whole sequence can be likened to a biological clock that is set and regulated by length of day.

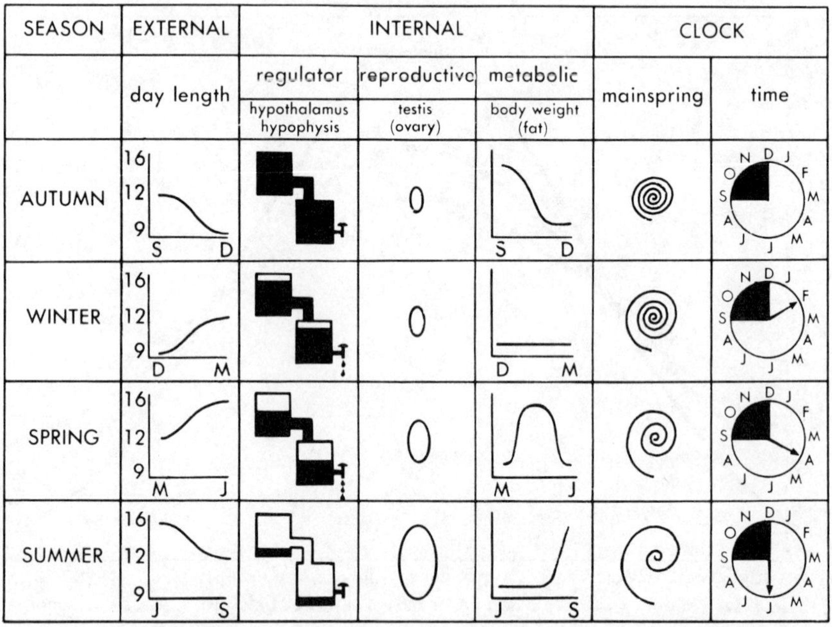

SEASON	EXTERNAL	INTERNAL			CLOCK	
	day length	regulator	reproductive	metabolic	mainspring	time
		hypothalamus hypophysis	testis (ovary)	body weight (fat)		
AUTUMN						
WINTER						
SPRING						
SUMMER						

Fig. 5-4. Factors involved in the photoperiod timing of spring migration in birds and an analogy with a clock. The daily light-dark cycle controls most of the activities of the internal regulators, the hypothalamus and the hypophysis (pituitary). The other internal changes are responses to the regulator. The face of the clock shows monthly time, and only the progressive phase is illustrated. The shaded portion of the clock indicates the preparatory phase. There is no doubt that migration is preceded by a change in physiological state, but it is not certain how this change actually releases the migratory behavior. (Redrawn from A. Wolfson, *Northwestern Tri-Quarterly,* Fall 1960.)

Among other seasonal activities that have been shown to be under photoperiod control are: flowering in many plants, elongation of stems in seedling plants, hibernation and seasonal change in hair coats in mammals, reproduction in many animals other than birds, and diapause (resting stage) in insects. In plants, day length acts through a pigment called phytochrome, which in turn activates enzymes controlling growth and flowering processes. It has even been shown that the number of underground nitrogen-fixing root nodules in legumes is controlled by photoperiod acting through the leaves of the plant. Since nitrogen-fixing bacteria in the nodules require food energy from the plant if they are to do their work, the more light and chlorophyll the more food for the bacteria; maximum coordination between the plant and its bacterial partners seems to be enhanced by the photoperiod regulator.

Insects that have two generations a year have evolved a neat day-length response that, as in birds, involves a neurohormone mechanism. Long days stimulate the "brain" (actually a nerve cord ganglion) to produce a hormone bringing on a diapause or resting egg, but short days do not have such an effect. Thus, individuals of the first generation hatched during the short days of spring produce eggs that immediately hatch into a second generation. Individuals in the second generation subjected to the long days of summer produce diapause eggs that do not hatch until the next spring, no matter how favorable temperature, moisture, and other conditions may be.

Light, of course, is not the only regulator. Seeds of many annual desert plants sprout only when there is a shower of a certain minimum magnitude (one-half inch of rain or more, for example); the mechanism here seems to involve a chemical germination inhibitor that must be washed out of the seed coat. These few examples will serve to emphasize the reciprocal relationships between organisms and their nonliving environment.

The Special Case of Fire as an Ecological Factor

Contrary to popular opinion, fire in nature is not a completely artificial factor created by man, nor is it always detrimental to man's interests. Fire is an important environmental factor in many terrestrial ecosystems and was important long before man attempted to control it. Because man can, within limits, control fire, it is especially important that he study this factor thoroughly, and with an objective mind. If we cannot learn to handle this relatively simple environmental factor in our own best interest, we have no business attempting to control rainfall or other vastly more complex matters.

Fire is both a limiting and a regulatory factor, as are most of the other factors we have discussed. It is important in warm or dry regions, and regions with warm and dry seasons such as in the southern third of the United States or in Central Africa. In such areas seasonal or periodic light fires apply selective pressure that favors the survival and growth of some species at the expense of others. Many natural communities in such regions are "fire types" in that their prosperity or very survival depends on fire. The effect of fire in one such community is shown in the sketches in Fig. 5-5. In this case the grass is not only adapted to fire but is much more valuable to man than the desert shrubs that tend to increase in the absence of fire. If man wants to keep fire out of such communities he must substitute something else in order to prevent a change to an economically less desirable vegetation. Chemicals may be effective, but they are much more expensive than "controlled" or "prescribed" burning as practiced, for example, in southeastern long-leafed pine forests, another fire-type ecosystem.

Although more work needs to be done in this area, it now appears that in dry or hot regions fire acts as a decomposer to bring about a release of mineral nutrients from accumulated old litter that becomes so dry that bacteria and fungi cannot act on it. Thus, fire may actually increase productivity by speeding up recycling. Certainly the big game herds of Africa or the deer in California chaparral (a shrub fire type) do not thrive unless periodic fires bring on a flush of new palatable grass or foliage. Furthermore, periodic light fires prevent the start of bad fires by keeping the combustible surface litter to a minimum. In southern California, for example, fire prevention in the chaparral vegetation has often resulted in severe fires that wipe out many homes.

It is extremely important that we distinguish between the light surface fires characteristic of the fire-type ecosystem and the wild forest fires of northern forests; the latter, of course, are all bad, since they destroy nearly the

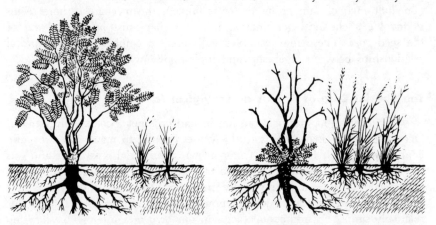

Fig. 5-5. Diagrams show how fire favors grass over mesquite shrubs in southwestern U.S. In the absence of fire the mesquite chokes out the grass (left). After a fire, grass recovers quickly, growing with increased vigor under conditions of reduced competition (right). Controlled burning will eliminate the mesquite entirely and maintain the grassland. (Redrawn with permission. Copyright © 1961 by *Scientific American*, Inc. All rights reserved.)

entire community. Because man, by his carelessness, tends to increase such holocausts, it is necessary that the public be made sharply aware of the necessity of fire prevention in forests. The intelligent citizen should recognize that he, as an individual, should never start or cause fires anywhere in nature; however, the scientific use of fire as a tool by trained persons is quite a different matter.

Pollution

Another set of limiting factors of special interest to man comes under the heading of pollution, a term rather loosely used to indicate substances introduced into the environment that are potentially harmful or that interfere with man's use of his environment. Water pollution by industrial and domestic wastes, air pollution (that is, "smog") and soil pollution (including excessive erosion) are three types of special concern. As with fire, pollution can be controlled to an advantage if man has the knowledge and the will to do so. We have already touched upon several ways in which ecological principles contribute to pollution problems, such as the use of diversity indices in assaying effects. The special case of radioactive pollutants was discussed in Chapter 4. There is no more important field of applied science than what we now call *environmental engineering,* in which ecology and engineering are combined in order to cope with the ever-increasing volume of man-made wastes.

From the limiting-factor standpoint we can make a fundamental distinction between two basic types of wastes: (1) those that involve an increase in volume or rate of introduction of materials already present in natural ecosystems, and (2) those involving poisons and chemicals that are not normally present in nature. In the former case there are adapted organisms and communities that can use and break down the material. Thus domestic sewage, which contains mostly organic matter and ordinary minerals (materials present in all ecosystems in low concentrations), is no real problem so long as ecosystems are not overloaded. The modern sewage disposal station consists of a chain of engineered ecosystems such as filter beds, oxidation ponds, etc., which enable adapted microflora and other organisms to reduce the organic load to a point where an ordinary stream can absorb the extra load without biological breakdown. In fact, the primary production is often increased. With poisons such as insecticides, many industrial chemicals, or components of "smog," however, there may be no organisms capable of using them and breaking them down into harmless forms should they reach excessive concentrations in air, streams, lakes, and soil; some of these poisons break down eventually, but a slow build-up often occurs (as in the case of strontium-90; see Chapter 4) that may not be noticed until too late. Man should make every effort to keep this class of pollutants out of the general environment.

SUGGESTED READING LIST

BECK, STANLEY D., "Insects and the length of the day," *Scientific American*, February 1960, pp. 108–118.

BULLOCK, T. H., "Compensation for temperature in the metabolism and activity of poikilotherms," *Biological Reviews*, Vol. 30 (1955), pp. 311–342.

CLARKE, GEORGE L., 1954. *Elements of ecology*. New York: Wiley. Chapter 8.

COOPER, CHARLES F., "The ecology of fire," *Scientific American*, April 1961, pp. 150–160.

DAUBENMIRE, R. F., 1959. *Plants and environment; a textbook of autecology*, 2d ed. New York: Wiley.

ELIASSEN, ROLF, "Stream pollution," *Scientific American*, March 1952, pp. 17–21.

HYNES, H. B. N., 1962. *The biology of polluted waters*. Liverpool, England: Liverpool University Press.

NAYLOR, AUBERY W., "The control of flowering," *Scientific American*, May 1952, pp. 49–56. SALISBURY, F. B., "The flowering process," *Scientific American*, April 1958, pp. 108–117. BULTLER, W. L., and DOWNS, R. J., "Light and plant development," *Scientific American*, December 1960, pp 56–63. These three articles trace discoveries that have been made as to how light or other environmental factors control plant reproduction and growth.

ODUM, EUGENE P., 1959. *Fundamentals of ecology*, 2d ed. Philadelphia: Saunders. Chapter 4.

RYTHER, JOHN H., "The Sargasso Sea," *Scientific American*, January 1956, pp. 98–104.

———, and GUILLARD, R. R., "Enrichment experiments as a means of studying nutrients limiting to phytoplankton production," *Deep-Sea Research*, Vol. 6 (1959), pp. 65–69.

WENT, FRITS W., "Climate and agriculture," *Scientific American*, June 1957, pp. 82–94.

WITHROW, R. B. (ed.), 1959. *Photoperiodism and related phenomena in plants and animals*, Publication No. 55, American Association for the Advancement of Science, Washington, D.C. (See especially articles on birds by Wolfson and Farner, pp. 679–750).

ZAREM, A. M., and RAND, W. E., "Smog," *Scientific American*, May 1952, pp. 15–19.

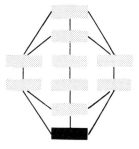

CHAPTER SIX

ECOLOGICAL

REGULATION We now come to the more purely biological

aspects of ecology, that is, the interaction of organisms with organisms in the maintenance of community structure and function. Up to this point much of our attention has been focused on the role of the great physical and chemical forces in the ecosystem. We have outlined how energy from the sun flows through the systems of nature such as the oceans, croplands, and forests. Likewise, we have demonstrated how materials are cycled and recycled, and how populations and communities are adapted and limited by temperature, light, and other abiotic factors. We have already emphasized that organisms are not just pawns in a great chess game in which the physical environment directs all the moves. Quite to the contrary, communities modify, change, and regulate their physical environment within certain limits; we have cited a number of examples in the previous chapters, as, for instance, bacterial regeneration of nitrogen, or the reef-building activities of cooperating teams of corals and algae. What we have not yet considered in detail are principles dealing with interactions of populations and their role in shaping the development of communities in time. This aspect of ecology we might designate as "ecoregulation" to go along with "ecoenergetics," and "ecocycling," the other major aspects already discussed.

ECOLOGICAL SUCCESSION

One of the most dramatic and important consequences of biological regulation in the community as a whole is the phenomenon of ecological succession. When a cultivated field is abandoned in the eastern part of North America, for example, the forest that originally occupied the site returns only after a series of temporary communities have prepared the way. The successive stages may be entirely different in structure and function from the forest that eventually develops on the site. In a sense, we may think of such temporary communities as developmental stages analogous to the life-history stages through which many organisms pass before reaching adulthood. Ecological succession, then, may be defined in terms of the following three parameters: (1) It is the orderly process of community changes; these are directional and, therefore, predictable. (2) It results from the modification of the physical environment by the community. (3) It culminates in the establishment of as stable an ecosystem as is biologically possible on the site in question. It is important to emphasize that ecological succession is *community controlled;* each set of organisms changes the physical substrate and the microclimate (local conditions of temperature, light, etc.), thereby making conditions favorable for another set of organisms. When the site has been modified as much as it can be by biological processes, a steady state develops—at least in theory. The species involved, time required, and degree of stability achieved depend on geography, climate, substrate, and other physical factors, but the process of succession itself is biological, not physical. That is, the physical environment determines the pattern of succession but does not cause it.

Some Basic Terms

In ecological terminology the developmental stages are known as *seral stages,* and the final steady state as the *climax.* The entire gradient of communities that is characteristic of a given site is called a *sere.* Succession that begins on a sterile area where conditions of existence are not at first favorable—as, for example, a newly exposed sand dune or a recent lava flow—is termed *primary succession.* The term *secondary succession* refers to community development on sites previously occupied by well-developed communities, or succession on sites where nutrients and conditions of existence are already favorable, such as abandoned croplands, plowed grasslands, cut-over forests, or new ponds. As would be expected, the rate of change is much more rapid, and the time required for the completion of the sere is much shorter, in secondary succession. Finally, it is important to distinguish between what may be called (for lack of better terms) *autotrophic succession* and *heterotrophic succession.* The former is the widespread type in nature that begins in a predominantly inorganic environment and is characterized by early and continued dominance by autotrophic organisms. Unless otherwise indicated, "ecological succession" in this chapter refers to the autotrophic type. Heterotrophic succession characterized by early dominance by heterotrophs occurs in the special case where the environment is predominantly organic as, for example, in a stream heavily polluted with sewage or, on a smaller scale, in a fallen log. Energy is maximum at the beginning and declines as succession occurs unless additional organic matter is imported or until an autotrophic regime takes over. In contrast, energy flow does not necessarily decline in the autotrophic type but is usually maintained or increased during succession.

A Simplified Model of Succession

Fig. 6-1 illustrates a very simple type of ecological succession that can be demonstrated in a laboratory experiment. The basic pattern shown here is the same as occurs in more complex succession under natural conditions. The particular diagram shown was suggested by the Spanish ecologist Dr. Ramon Margalef; hence we may call it the "Margalef model of succession." The purpose of a model is to simplify the situation sufficiently to bring out principles and suggest hypotheses that, in turn, can be tested in the more complex situations of real nature.

At the top of the diagram in Fig. 6-1 is a series of culture flasks containing plankton communities in different stages of succession. The graph below shows changes in two aspects of structure and two aspects of function. The first flask to the left contains an old and relatively stable community; this flask represents the climax in our model. Diversity of species is high

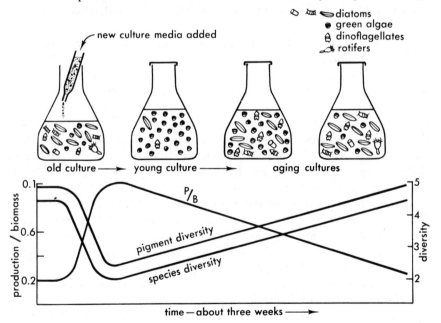

Fig. 6-1. A laboratory model illustrating ecological succession. The old culture at the left is characterized by a variety of species and pigments (high diversity) but a low ratio of net production to biomass (P/B). When fresh culture medium is added, succession is set in motion. The first stage, or the young culture, is characterized by dominance of a few species (hence low diversity) and a relatively high rate of net production. (After Margalef.)

in the climax; species of diatoms, green flagellates, dinoflagellates, and rotifers are shown in the diagram to illustrate the variety of plants and animals that might be present. The biochemical diversity is also high, as indicated by the variety of plant pigments. Dr. Margalef has found that if pigments are extracted with acetone from a sample of the community and the optical density of the extracted materials determined in a spectrophotometer (as described in Chapter 2; see Fig. 2-2), the ratio of optical density at the wavelength 430 mμ to that at 665 mμ provides an index to pigment diversity. The 430 band represents the yellow pigments, which vary with different species of plants and animals, and the 665 band represents chlorophyll a, a predominant photosynthetic pigment. The 430/665 ratio, which we might call the "yellow/green" ratio, tends to be high—perhaps between 3 and 5—in the old, stable ecosystem.

The other two curves in Fig. 6-1 depict metabolic and biomass relationships. In the old culture the ratio of gross production of the community to total respiration of the community (that is, respiration of both plants and animals), which we can call the P/R ratio, tends to approach 1. That is, all food manufactured tends to be used up, on the average. Consequently, net production tends to be small and the ratio of net production to biomass (the P/B curve in Fig. 6-1) is low.

If we now add fresh culture medium (containing inorganic nutrients and growth substances) to the old culture, as shown in Fig. 6-1, ecological succession is set in motion. (The same effect could be obtained by starting a new culture.) An early stage of succession is shown in the second flask. In contrast to the old culture, species diversity is low; often one or two species of phytoplankton are dominant. Green algae or diatoms may assume dominance in the early stages of succession not only in cultures but often in natural waters. Chlorophyll predominates, so that the 430/665 ratio drops to about 2, indicating low biochemical diversity. On the other hand, gross production now exceeds community respiration, so that the ratio P/R is greater than 1. Likewise, the ratio of net production to standing crop biomass becomes higher. In other words, autotrophy greatly exceeds heterotrophy in the pioneer or early succession stage. The two flasks on the right side of the diagram show the gradual return to the climax, or steady state, where autotrophy tends to balance heterotrophy. For the purposes of subsequent discussion we may think of the pioneer stages as "young nature" and the climax as "old nature."

As indicated in the previous section, succession may proceed either from the extremely autotrophic condition where P exceeds R, as in the cultures we have just described, or from the extremely heterotrophic condition where R exceeds P (or where P may be zero). An interesting culture model of the heterotrophic type of succession is the familiar hay infusion often used for growing protozoans and other small animals for students to study in the elementary biology laboratory. If a quantity of dried hay is boiled, and the solution allowed to stand a few days, a thriving culture of heterotrophic bacteria develops. If some pond water containing seed stocks of various small animals is then added to the hay infusion, a succession of species can be observed for about a month. Usually, small flagellates called monads appear first, followed in rapid succession by ciliated protozoans such as Colpoda and Paramecium; changes then come more slowly, with specialized ciliates (such as Hypotricha and Vorticella), Amoeba, or rotifers reaching peaks of abundance. If algae get into the culture, then an equilibrium with P nearing R may be approached; otherwise the culture will run down in about 90 days since all the organisms will die for lack of food, the original organic matter introduced having been used up.

Thus, the two types of succession can be contrasted on a small scale in the laboratory, or as a class exercise in a course in ecology, by an algae culture on inorganic media and a hay infusion. Such cultures demonstrate, respectively, what happens in the early stages of succession in a new pond or artificial lake, and in the early stages of succession following dumping of sewage or other organic wastes into a pond or stream. Laboratory cultures are much too small for the study of equilibrium conditions, however, since they do not contain enough diversity (biological or physical) for the development of effective self-regulation.

The Major Trends and Causes of Succession

A more general and complete summary of important changes in community structure and function in the sere is shown in Table 6-1.

Expected trends in the gradient from young to old nature are grouped under three headings: species structure, organic structure, and energy flow (community metabolism). Although ecologists have studied succession in many parts of the world, most of the emphasis to date has been on the descriptive aspects such as the qualitative changes in species structure. Only recently have the functional aspects of succession also been considered. Consequently, some of the items listed in Table 6-1 must be considered hypothetical in the sense that they are based on good experimental or theoretical evidence, but have not been verified by adequate data from the field. Four aspects seem most significant and require a bit more explanation as follows:

(1) *The kinds of plants and animals change continuously with succession;* those species that are important in the pioneer stages are not likely to be important in the climax. When the density of species in a sere is plotted against time, a characteristic stair-step graph is obtained, as illustrated by Fig. 6-2. Such a pattern usually is apparent whether we are considering a specific taxonomic group such as birds or a trophic group such

TABLE 6-1

A Tabular Model for Ecological Succession
(of the Autotrophic Type)

Ecosystem characteristic	Trend in succession: early stage to climax or young to old nature
SPECIES STRUCTURE	
Species composition	changes rapidly at first, then more gradually
Number species of autotrophs	increases in primary and often early in secondary succession; may decline in older stages
Number species of heterotrophs	increases until relatively late in the sere
Species diversity	increases initially, then becomes stabilized or declines in older stages
ORGANIC STRUCTURE	
Total biomass	increases
Nonliving organic matter	increases
Chlorophylls	increase during early phase of primary succession; little or no increase during secondary succession
Pigment diversity	increases, at least early in the sere
ENERGY FLOW (COMMUNITY METABOLISM)	
Food-chain relationships (food webs)	become more complex [a]
Gross production	increases during early phase of primary succession; little or no increase during secondary succession
Net community production	decreases
Community respiration	increases
P/R ratio	$P > R$ to $P = R$

[a] In terms of "information theory" the total information in the community increases, which means that the number of possible interactions between species, individuals, and materials increases during succession.

Time in years	1-10	10-25	25-100	100+
Community type	grassland	shrubs	pine forest	hardwood forest

Grasshopper sparrow
Meadowlark
Field sparrow
Yellowthroat
Yellow-breasted chat
Cardinal
Towhee
Bachman's sparrow
Prairie warbler
White-eyed vireo
Pine warbler
Summer tanager
Carolina wren
Carolina chickadee
Blue-gray gnatcatcher
Brown-headed nuthatch
Wood pewee
Hummingbird
Tufted titmouse
Yellow-throated vireo
Hooded warbler
Red-eyed vireo
Hairy woodpecker
Downy woodpecker
Crested flycatcher
Wood thrush
Yellow-billed cuckoo
Black and white warbler
Kentucky warbler
Acadian flycatcher

Number of common species[a]	2	8	15	19
Density (pairs per 100 acres)	27	123	113	233

[a] A common species is arbitrarily designated as one with a density of 5 pairs per 100 acres or greater in one or more of the 4 community types.

Fig. 6-2. The general pattern of secondary succession on abandoned farmland in the southeastern United States. The upper diagram shows four stages in the life form of the vegetation (grassland, shrubs, pines, hardwoods) while the bar graph shows changes in passerine bird population that accompany the changes in autotrophs. A similar pattern will be found in any area where a forest is climax, but the species of plants and animals that take part in the development series will vary according to the climate or topography of the area. (Redrawn from D. W. Johnston and E. P. Odum, *Ecology*, Vol. 37, 1956.)

as herbivores or producers. Typically, some species in the gradient have wider tolerances or niche preferences than others and, therefore, persist over a longer period of time. In general, the more species in the group (whether taxonomic or ecological) that are geographically available for colonization, the more restricted will be the occurrence of each species in the time sequence. This kind of regulatory adjustment is the result of competition, which we shall discuss in more detail later in this chapter.

(2) *Biomass and the standing crop of organic matter increase with succession.* As indicated in the discussion of pigments, the variety as well as the amount of biochemicals (that is, organic materials of biological significance) apparently increase with the accumulation of many kinds of organic materials in the environment. In both aquatic and terrestrial environments decomposing organic materials or humus (see Chapter 2) tend to increase with time. Also, many soluble substances accumulate; these include sugars, amino acids, and many others that as yet have been scarcely identified. Natural bodies of water that are well along in the successional process often contain as much organic matter in solution as is present in the bodies of living organisms. Likewise, organic extrusions from roots of forest trees may be considerable. These liquid productions that leak out from the bodies of organisms are usually known as *extrametabolites*. Some of these substances provide food for microorganisms, and perhaps also for macroorganisms; the extent to which animals (as, for example, zooplankton or soil arthropods) can use soluble organic food is controversial at present. Other substances are equally important in that they may act as inhibitors (antibiotics) or as growth promoters (as, for example, vitamins). It has been repeatedly shown that dense cultures of some species of algae produce substances that inhibit their growth, thus providing a potential self-regulating mechanism. Likewise, when oysters are densely cultured in a shallow bay, accumulation of organic extrametabolites in the sediments eventually reduces their growth. That substances produced by one organism may inhibit other completely different species was dramatically brought to our attention by the discovery of penicillin and other bacterial antibiotics produced by fungi. Another example is the poisonous "red tides" that occasionally develop in coastal waters when extrametabolites toxic to fish are produced by dense populations of dinoflagellates; study of these exaggerated situations in nature is helping us understand the role of antibiotics in more normal situations. In other cases, increasing organic matter stimulates the growth of bacteria that manufacture vitamin B_{12}, a necessary growth promoter for many animals (many are unable to manufacture this and other vitamins themselves). Ecologists are now engaged in lively discussions as to whether growth and inhibitory substances, such as those mentioned, are concentrated enough to be important under the less crowded conditions of most natural ecosystems. The point to be made here is that extrametabolites will tend to increase, at least in variety, with

succession, not only because there is increasing diversity of production but also because accumulation of organic matter often produces temporary or permanent local anaerobic conditions that favor the persistence of incompletely decomposed organic substances. If such substances do prove to be regulatory, then we would be justified in calling these substances *environmental hormones.* There is no logical reason why hormones (that is, chemical regulators) may not be important at the ecosystem level as well as the cell level. Chemical regulation is one way of achieving community stability as the climax is approached. Finally, since the physical (as, for example, light and water relations) as well as the chemical nature of the environment are modified by the changing organic structure, there is no question that *the increase in amount of and the change in organic structure are two of the main factors bringing about the succession of species.*

3. *The diversity of species tends to increase with succession,* at least initially, although it is not clear from the present data that the change in variety of taxa follows the same pattern in all ecosystems. Increase in diversity of heterotrophs is especially striking; the variety of microorganisms and heterotrophic plants and animals is likely to be much greater in the later stages of succession than in the early stages. Maximum diversity of autotrophs in many ecosystems seems to be reached earlier in succession. The enlargement of organic structure, as outlined above, is, of course, related in a cause-and-effect manner to the increase in species diversity; as biomass increases, stratification and zonation create many new habitat niches (litter, humus, bark, dead wood, etc., in a forest). It should be emphasized that we are here considering *diversity in terms of the community as a whole or in terms of some functional group* (such as herbivores), *and not in terms of a limited taxonomic group.* As outlined in item (1), the kinds of organisms may be expected to change with succession no matter what their taxonomic group. But it does not follow that the diversity of a limited taxonomic group will necessarily increase with succession. Thus, the number of species of insects of the order Orthoptera (grasshoppers, etc.) present will likely be greatest in the early herbaceous stages of a forest succession rather than in the climax forest, because the majority of species in this group happen to be adapted to the grassland type of habitat. On the other hand, if we count all species of grazing herbivores regardless of their order, class, or phylum, we would likely find greater diversity in the later stages. The interplay of opposite trends makes it difficult to generalize. The increase in size of individual organisms and the increase in competition for space and resources tend to reduce diversity of species, while the increase in niches tends to increase it. Even where species diversity declines, more biological "information" is stored in the enlarged organic structure presumably enhancing stability and thermodynamic efficiency in the preservation of maximum biomass.

4. *A decrease in net community production and a corresponding increase in community respiration are two of the most striking and important trends in succession.* As indicated in Table 6-1, gross production may be expected to increase in the early stages of primary succession, with little or no change evident in later stages or in secondary succession. Perhaps the best way to picture this over-all trend is as follows: *species, biomass, and the P/R ratio continue to change long after the maximum gross primary production possible for the site has been achieved.* As one evidence for this we may cite the situation in regard to leaves in a terrestrial broad-leaved forest succession. Agricultural scientists have repeatedly found that maximum productivity of broad-leaved crops occurs when the leaf surface area exposed to the incoming light from above is about 4 or 5 times the surface area of the ground. Any increase in leaves beyond this level does not increase the photosynthetic rate per square meter, since increased shading conceals any advantage that might accrue from increased photosynthetic tissue. In fact, the increased respiration of the extra leaves that do not receive adequate light may reduce the net production of the crop. In a forest the leaf area apparently continues to increase far beyond that limit experimentally shown to increase gross production, since leaf area per ground surface area is often 10 or more in an old forest. Since forests are among the most successful of ecosystems with a long geological history of survival, we may well consider the possibility that the extra leaves have other important functions in the ecosystem in addition to production (they may help regulate temperature, for example).

The Time Factor in Succession

The changes shown in Figs. 6-1, 6-2, and Table 6-1 seem to be typical of all succession regardless of geographical location or type of ecosystem. Community structure and physical environment mainly affect (1) the time required, that is, whether the horizontal scale (x axis Figs. 6-1, 6-2) is measured in weeks, months, or years, and (2) the relative stability of the climax. Thus, in open-water systems, as in cultures, the community is able to modify the physical environment to only a small extent. Consequently, succession in such ecosystems, if it occurs at all, is brief, perhaps lasting for only a few weeks. In a typical marine pond or marine bay, for example, a brief succession from diatoms to dinoflagellates occurs each season, or perhaps several times during a season. A climax, if it can be said to occur, has a limited life span. In a forest ecosystem, to take the other extreme, a large biomass gradually accumulates with time and the community continues to change. If we refer again to Fig. 3-2 (p. 43), which contrasts the structure and energy flow of a forest and a marine community, we can easily see why the very large biological structure of the forest enables that community to buffer the physical environment and to change the substrate and micro-climate to a much greater extent than is possible in a marine situation.

Recent studies on primary succession on such sites as sand dunes or recent lava flows indicate that at least 1000 years may be required for the development of a climax. Secondary succession on cut-over forest land or abandoned agricultural land is more rapid, but at least 200 years may be required for development of a mature forest in a moist, temperate climate. When the climate or another physical factor is more severe, as in desert, tundra, or grassland regions, the duration of the sere may be short, since the community cannot modify the harsh physical environment to any large extent. Secondary succession in grasslands, for example, may require less than half a century. Consequently, a complete sere on a given site can be observed by a man during his lifetime. Although the species of plants vary geographically, a pattern of four stages has been repeatedly described on abandoned croplands or old wagon roads of the plains of central and western North America: (1) annual weed stage (2 to 5 years), (2) short-lived grass stage (3 to 10 years), (3) early perennial grass stage (10 to 20 years), and climax grass stage (reached in 20 to 40 years).

Where a long period of time is required to complete the sere, climatic cycles, storms, severe fires, etc., are likely to interfere sooner or later, hence in actual practice long-term successions are not completely directional or predictable. It follows from what we have outlined that more mature suc-cessional stages will be more resistant, but by no means immune, to periodic surges in physical forces so long as these forces are not completely catastrophic to life. Thus, a one-year drought has a very great effect on an early stage of succession or on a crop of corn or wheat, but much less effect on a climax forest or grassland. Only if the drought continues for several years would the climax begin to show appreciable changes. In the case of grassland, Dr. J. E. Weaver and his associates at the University of Nebraska have described in detail the changes in species structure and density of the stand that occur in a series of dry years; in general, the mature grassland tends to be set back to a somewhat earlier successional stage containing more annuals and short-lived perennials. However, a rapid recovery occurs on the return of a wet cycle. During the severe droughts of the mid-1930's on the Great Plains of the United States, healthy, mature grasslands, although stressed, were able to survive as intact communities and to hold down the soil, in sharp contrast to the complete biological collapse and severe wind erosion that occurred on croplands and overgrazed areas.

Stability of the Climax

While it is clear that the climax is relatively stable and can exist for a relatively long time as compared with the pioneer stages, it is not known if any community can be completely self-perpetuated and permanent, even assuming no change in the regional climate. As indicated in the previous section, this may be more of an academic than a practical question since catastrophes, whether natural storms or man-made bulldozers, are likely to shorten the life span of any community. Observations in very old forests suggest that self-destructive biological changes may be occurring, which, in the individual, we would call aging. Thus, young trees may not be quite replacing the old ones as they die, or regeneration of nutrients may be lagging and the whole metabolism thus slowing down. There are few data at present, but one wonders if communities may not suffer gradual aging after reaching maturity, just as do individual organisms. Storms and disease, of course, could hasten the aging and death of a climax and its replacement by a young, perhaps different, community. Now that radioactive tracers are available, the ecologist of the future should be able to study this problem and find out if mineral cycling and energy flow rates are slowing down in the climax.

The Significance of Ecological Succession

To summarize, the mature community with its greater diversity, larger organic structure, and balanced energy flows is often able to buffer the physical environment to a greater extent than the young community, which, however, is often the more productive. Thus, the achievement of a measure of stability or homeostasis, rather than a mere increase in productivity, in a fluctuating physical environment may well be the primary purpose (that is, the survival value) of ecological succession when viewed from the evolutionary standpoint.

The principles of ecological succession are of the greatest importance to mankind. Man must have early successional stages as a source of food, since he must have a large net primary production to harvest; in the climax community, because production is mostly consumed by respiration (plant and animal), net community production in an annual cycle may be zero. On the other hand, the stability of the climax and its ability to buffer and control physical forces (such as water and temperature) are desirable characteristics from the viewpoint of the human population. The only way man can have both a productive and a stable environment is to insure that a good mixture of early and mature successional stages are maintained, with interchanges of energy and materials. Excess food produced in young communities helps feed older stages that in return supply regenerated nutrients and help buffer the extremes of weather (storms, floods, etc.).

In the most stable and productive natural situation there is usually such a combination of successional stages. For example, in areas such as the inland sea of Japan or Long Island Sound, the young communities of plankton feed older, more stable communities on the rocks and on the bottom (benthic communities). The large biomass structure and diversity of the benthic communities provide not only habitat and shelter for life-history stages of pelagic forms but also regenerated nutrients necessary for continued productivity of the plankton. A similar, favorable situation exists in many terrestrial landscapes where productive croplands on the plains are intermingled with diverse forests and orchards on the hills and mountains. The crop fields are, ecologically speaking, "young nature" in that they are maintained as such by the constant labor of the farmer and his machines. The forests represent older, more diverse, and self-sustaining communities that have lower rates of net production but do not require the constant attention of man. It is important that both types of ecosystems be considered together in proper relation. If the forests are destroyed merely for the temporary gain in wood production, water and soil may wash down from the slopes and reduce the productivity of the plains. Forests have other values to mankind in addition to wood products; they should not be considered as crops in the sense of wheat or corn. The conservationist speaks of this as "multiple use," but unfortunately he often does not have the quantitative data to translate long-term uses into dollars. Consequently, too often the possibility for immediate economic gain in harvest overrides what later turns out to be more important. Part of the fault lies with ecologists, who have not provided enough concrete data on the importance of mature-type ecosystems in stabilizing water, nutrient, and other important environmental factors.

All we can say at present is that it would be very dangerous to convert our biosphere into one vast sheet of crops; it would also be a very dull world esthetically. For our own safety and protection, some definite percent of the landscape should be occupied by more or less natural communities. Just what this percentage should be in different climatic zones is unknown. We do know that when man thinks only of production he goes too far in stripping the landscape. Ruins of civilizations and man-made deserts in various parts of the world stand as evidence that man has not been aware of his heterotrophic nature and the need to adapt to nature as he attempts to control it. In many cases a shortage of water seems to have been the final cause of disaster for mankind.

BIOLOGICAL CONTROL AT THE POPULATION LEVEL

In the introduction of Chapter 5 we referred to four factors—energy, materials, conditions, and community—as being the primary regulators of nature. So far in this chapter we have discussed how the stage of succession may affect the numbers and diversity of organisms in an ecosystem. These primary factors are also important at the population level. In other words, if we became interested in a certain species, perhaps because it is of direct importance to man, we would need to consider how all of the primary factors affect that species. Often it turns out that energy, a specific physical factor, or a stage in succession is the major limiting or regulating factor. Furthermore, we may often apply such knowledge to increasing or decreasing the productivity of the species (assuming for the moment that it is in man's best interest to do so). For example, we may be able to increase the number of food or game fish in a pond by increasing the rate of primary production; or we may be able to reduce the number of a particular species of mosquito by modifying the conditions of existence in the aquatic environment of the larvae; or we may be able to control the number of Virginia deer by controlling the stage in ecological succession, since this species of deer thrives best in the early stages of forest succession. Note that in all three of these examples control might be brought about without direct action being taken for or against individuals of the species itself. Primary regulations of these sorts are like the coarse adjustments on microscopes or other instruments: they set the general and often rather wide limits within which a given population may function. There are other factors at the population level that may act as additional coarse adjustments or more particularly as fine adjustments that dampen oscillations.

Very frequently, secondary considerations involving interactions within the population, or within a group of closely associated species, are strongly limiting or controlling. In such cases, the size of the population may remain considerably below what the ecosystem could support were there no such internal limitations. In Chapter 3 we mentioned that the number of grazing insects in a forest is normally quite small in terms of available food and other conditions. In many cases, but in by no means all, it has been shown that parasites or predators are responsible for the limitation.

The study of population interactions and the role they may play in determining the population size of specific organisms has become one of the most active areas of research in ecology—and one of the most controversial. Controversy stems mostly from a lack of good data, but sometimes from too narrow a viewpoint. In making a detailed study of a particular species it is especially important not to forget primary ecosystem limitations that set the outside limits. In real life both the coarse (that is, ecosystem) and the fine adjustments (that is, population) are important, but *their relative importance may vary greatly according to the circumstance.*

Before we can go further into this important subject we shall need to cover a few points of special interest to the population ecologist.

Population Attributes

A population, as you recall from Chapter 1, is defined as the collective group of organisms of a particular kind in the community. In practice, a population is simply all of the organisms of the same species found oc-cupying a given space. A population is a unique level of organization be-cause it has a number of important group properties shared neither by in-dividuals in the population nor by the community. The more important of these population characteristics, or group attributes, are as follows:

Density—population size in relation to a unit of space.

Birth rate, or more broadly, natality (so as to include organisms that arise from seeds, spores, eggs, etc.)—the rate at which new individuals are added to the population by reproduction.

Death rate, or *mortality*—the rate at which individuals are lost by death.

Age distribution—the proportion of individuals of different ages in the group.

Population dispersion—the way in which individuals are distributed in space.

Population growth rate or *growth form*—the net result of natality, mor-tality, and dispersal (immigration and emigration) from the group.

Individual organisms are born, die, have age, and grow, but such characteristics as birth rate, death rate, density, and the others listed above are meaningful only at the group level. If we are to understand thoroughly the ecology of a species, we must study and measure these population group characteristics as well as know the life history and identifying features of the species.

It is quite evident that the degree of crowding, or density, and the pattern of dispersion of individuals (whether random, uniform, or clumped together in a limited area) are especially important in determining the degree of interaction between individuals of the same or other species. Not so evident is the role that the type of population growth plays in biological control. Some populations tend to be self-limited in that the rate of growth decreases as the density increases. Such populations tend to level off in density before saturation, and their population growth can be said to be in-versely *density dependent*. Other populations are not self-limited but tend to grow in geometric sequence (for example, 2, 4, 8, 16, 32, etc.) unless or until checked by forces outside of the population (that is, other popula-tions or general ecosystem limitations); such populations may overshoot their energy and habitat resources, literally eating themselves out of food and home. Their population growth can be said to be *density independent,* at least until the density becomes very great. When poorly regulated by factors outside of the population itself, species of the latter type are subject to severe oscillations in density and may become serious pests to man.

There is still a third type of relationship between density and growth rate. In some species the reproductive rate is greater at intermediate density than at either low or high density; in other words, both "undercrowding" and "overcrowding" are limiting. Such a pattern is called the "Allee growth type" after the late W. C. Allee (see Suggested Reading List at the end of this chapter). Some species of sea gulls are good examples. Most sea gulls nest in colonies on isolated islands or other protected places. In certain species it has been shown that the number of young produced per pair is greater when the density of the breeding colony is fairly large than when only a few pairs are present or when there is severe crowding. In highly social species, behavior patterns necessary for pair formation and efficient care of the young are apparently stimulated and augmented by the nearby presence of other individuals. Oysters are also more successful when the local density is moderately high, but for another reason. The oyster begins its life as a planktonic larvae that must settle on some suitable hard substrate if it is to survive. Where a large number of old oysters are present in a colony their shells provide a favorable place for the settling of the larvae. When man greatly reduces the oyster colonies by "overfishing," population growth becomes so low that the colony recovers very slowly (or perhaps not at all), even though no longer "fished" and even though there are planktonic larvae present in the water. Thus, conservation of oysters or other species that exhibit low growth rate at low density depends on maintaining a large standing crop at all times.

The three patterns of growth rate in relation to density are diagramed in Fig. 6-3. Note that the growth rate per unit of population (that is, per individual, pair, 100 individuals, or other convenient unit), and not the total growth rate, is plotted against total density. Thus, in the inverse density-dependent or self-limiting type the number of individuals added to the population per individual per unit of time decreases as the density increases (curve 1 in Fig. 6-3). In the density-independent or nonself-limiting type the growth rate per individual continues at a high level until

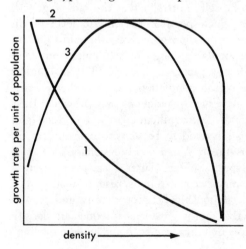

Fig. 6-3. Three patterns of population growth rate in relation to population density. 1: The growth rate decreases as density increases (self-limiting or inverse density-dependent type). 2: Growth rate remains high until density become high and factors outside of the population become limiting (density-independent type). 3: Growth rate is highest at intermediate densities (the Allee type).

a high density is reached (curve 2 in Fig. 6-3); that is, growth of the whole population is geometric, until a high density is reached. Finally, the Allee type is shown in curve 3 (Fig. 6-3); in this case growth rate per individual is at first directly density dependent and then inversely density dependent with optimum (for population growth rate) at an intermediate density. As with some previous diagrams in this book the curves in Fig. 6-3 are intended to serve as general graphic models for the range of relationships to be found in nature. Intermediate situations would be expected, especially between patterns 1 and 2.

Among species with high reproductive potential, lemmings, which are small, mouselike rodents, are famous for "population irruptions" that occur every three or four years in the arctic. Another well-documented case of unstable populations involves needle-eating caterpillars (larvae of moths) in German pure-pine forests. Between 1880 and 1940 outbreaks of one or more species occurred every 5 to 10 years, when as many as 10,000 pupae per 1000 square meters were present (producing enough caterpillars to defoliate the trees temporarily) as compared with the "normal" density of less than 1 in 1000 m². On the other hand, the size of most populations, even those with high reproductive potentials, remains remarkably constant year after year. As we have already pointed out, there is a general correlation between diversity and stability on the ecosystem level and homeostatsis at the population level. That is, irruptions and outbreaks are more likely to occur where the biological structure is simplified, either by man or by severe natural limiting factors. We assume, but without real evidence, that greater diversity means more feedback and hence closer control. Even in stable ecosystems, however, an occasional species will irrupt. One thing we can say for certain: we do not know enough about the details of population regulation to do a very good job of predicting when or where some species will break out of its usual limits.

Competition

The word "competition" denotes a striving for the same thing. At the ecological level competition becomes important when two organisms strive for something that is not in adequate supply for both of them. Thus, plants compete for light and nutrients in a forest, and animals compete for food and shelter when the latter are relatively scarce in terms of the density of animals. If the population consists of only a few scattered individuals, competition will not be a factor of ecological importance. In the arctic, for example, plants may be so few and scattered due to the severe climate that no competition for light occurs.

The result of competition is that both parties (that is, the competitors) are hampered in some manner. At the population level this means that density, or rate of population energy flow, will be reduced or held in check by the competitive action. There is another type of interaction, known as mutual inhibition, that has the same result. This occurs when two organisms interfere with one another while striving for something even though that something is not in short supply. For example, the organisms might secrete substances that interfere with each other; or they might even eat each other. Many ecologists prefer not to include such direct mutual inhibition under the heading of competition. Since, however, we are interested in the results of interactions in terms of the community, we are perhaps justified in lumping all reciprocal negative interactions under the heading of competition.

Both intraspecific and interspecific competition can be very important in determining the kinds and numbers of organisms. Intraspecific competition is an important factor in those populations that tend to be self-regulated in the manner described above. An interesting behavior pattern, which results in intraspecific competition for space and a rather effective control of population size, is known as *territoriality*; it is characteristic of many species of birds and some other higher animals. At the beginning of the breeding season the male of a territorial species of bird will "stake out" a definite area of its habitat (that is, the "territory") and defend it against other males of the same species, with the result that no other male is allowed to enter the area. Much of the loud bird song one hears in the spring is for the purpose of announcing to other males "ownership" of land, and not for the purpose of wooing the female, as is often supposed. A male that is successful in holding its land has a high probability of mating and nesting, while a male that is unable to establish such a territory will not breed. Once the pair is formed, the female also joins in the defense of the territory in many species. The defended territory also serves a positive purpose of insuring that the complex business of caring for the nest and young will not be interrupted by the presence of other males and females. Finally, it should be mentioned that the actual defense of the territory does not usually involve much actual fighting or other severe stress. Would-be invaders respect the established bird; loud song or threat displays usually are sufficient to cause the invader to withdraw. However, if one of the pair should be killed it is very often quickly replaced by a bird from a reservoir of individuals not established. Therefore, since the territorial behavior pattern helps avoid both overcrowding and undercrowding it can be said to be regulatory.

In some species intraspecific control of population size seems to begin before there is severe competition for energy, materials, or space. For example, intraspecific fighting and other stress in some mammals reduce the reproductive rate before food or habitat becomes limiting; in other words, individuals do not tolerate crowding even when there is plenty to eat. Something similar may occur in desert plant communities. As one drives through the desert in the southwestern United States one is impressed with the fact that desert shrubs are widely spaced, often almost uniformly distributed as if planted at regularly spaced intervals. The pattern would seem to be explained by competition for scarce water, which eliminates all but one individual in a given area. However, evolution of self-regulation of the population has occurred in some species, in that severe competition for water is avoided by the production of leaf or root hormones that inhibit development of other individuals in the neighborhood. That is, chemical substances released by decaying leaves that fall to the ground under the shrub, or by the living roots in the soil inhibit or kill any seedlings that may start to sprout. Such a control mechanism would tend to keep plants spaced apart, thereby reducing actual competition for water, which might result in stunting or death of all plants should there be many trying to grow in the same place.

Interspecific Competition

Where there are two or more closely related species adapted to the same or similar niche, interspecific competition becomes important. If the competition is severe, one of the species may be eliminated completely, or forced into another niche or another geographical location; or the species involved may be able to live together at reduced density by sharing the resources in some sort of equilibrium.

One of the most thorough-going and long-term experimental studies of interspecific competition is that being carried out in the laboratory of Dr. Thomas Park at the University of Chicago. Dr. Park, his students, and associates work with flour beetles, especially species belonging to the genus *Tribolium*. These small beetles can complete their entire life history in a very simple and homogeneous habitat, namely, a jar of flour or wheat bran. The medium in this case is both food and habitat for larvae and adults. If fresh medium is added at regular intervals, a population of beetles can be maintained for a very long time. In the energy-flow terminology discussed in Chapter 3 this experimental set-up may be described as a stabilized heterotrophic ecosystem in which imports of food energy equal respiratory losses.

The investigators have found that when two different species of *Tribolium* are placed in this homogeneous little universe, invariably one species is eliminated sooner or later while the other one continues to thrive. In other words, one species always "wins" in the competition; or to put it another way, two species of *Tribolium* cannot both survive in the particular simple ecosystem. The relative number of individuals of each species originally placed into the culture does not affect the eventual outcome, but the "climate" imposed on the ecosystem does have a great effect on which species of a pair wins out. In Table 6-2 are shown the results of competition with two species, *Tribolium castaneum* and *Tribolium confusum,* at six different combinations of temperature and humidity. These data are based on 20 to 30 replicates at each condition. Prior to the experiments it had been found that each species could maintain a population at any of the six climates, provided it was alone in the culture; as already indicated, the two species cannot coexist in the limited universe, hence one or the other wins out when both are introduced into the same culture. As shown in Table 6-2, *T. castaneum* won out in all of the replications under hot-wet conditions while *T. confusum* always won under cool-dry conditions. Under intermediate conditions, sometimes one, sometimes the other species won, with the percentage of wins and losses following the gradient between the extreme conditions. Somewhere between the conditions of "warm-dry" and "warm-wet" the probability of either species winning might be 0.50, or 50 percent.

Dr. Park and his associates are not yet sure they understand just why the experiments come out the way they do. Obviously, *T. castaneum* is better adapted to high temperature and high humidity while *T. confusum* has some kind of advantage at low temperature and low humidity. The investigators can predict with a high degree of certainty that one species will win, and they can predict which species will win at the extremes of the climatic gradient; but at intermediate conditions they have not been able to predict which one will win in any given test (that is, they can

TABLE 6-2

Results of Interspecific Competition between Populations of
Two Species of Flour Beetles *(Tribolium)*

Climate	Temperature (°C)	Relative humidity (%)	Results of interspecific competition (%) [a]	
			Tribolium castaneum wins	*Tribolium confusum* wins
Hot-wet	34	70	100	0
Hot-dry	34	30	10	90
Warm-wet	29	70	86	14
Warm-dry	29	30	13	87
Cool-wet	24	70	31	69
Cool-dry	24	30	0	100

Data from Thomas Park, *Physiological Zoology,* Vol. 28 (1954), pp. 177–238.
[a] 20 to 30 replicate experiments for each of the six conditions. Each species can survive at any of the climates when alone in the culture, but only one species survives when both are present in the culture. The percentages indicate the proportion of replicates in which each species remained after elimination of the other species.

only predict on the basis of a certain probability). Population attributes, as measured in one-species cultures, help explain some of the outcome of competitive interaction. For example, the species with the highest population growth rate (under the conditions of existence in question) was usually found to win if the differences in growth rate were rather large. If growth rates differed only moderately, the one with the highest rate did not always win. The presence of a virus or other inhibitor in one species could easily tip the balance. Also, the investigators suspect that genetic strains within the species differ greatly in "competitive ability"; they are now hard at work exploring this possibility.

Species do not have to belong to what taxonomists consider the same genus to get involved in severe competition. Two species of different genera or even different families sometimes have very similar niche relations (recall that an ecological niche is, by definition, a functional position and not just a physical position in the ecosystem), and thus may compete for some limited resource. Forest trees, for example, although belonging to many different genera, may have very similar requirements for light and water and hence be in active competition where the density is high. Returning briefly to flour beetles, another investigator (Crombie, *J. Animal Ecol.*, 16, 1947:44) has found that *Tribolium* eliminates *Oryzaephilus* when both are in the same culture. In this case the larger larvae of *Tribolium* actively prey on the small larvae of the other species. When small glass tubes were mixed with the flour, however, both species were able to coexist, since the larvae of *Oryzaephilus* could take shelter in the tubes until they were large enough to escape being eaten. In this experimental ecosystem a sort of second habitat was created that enabled the two species to survive together. In general, we can say that interspecific competition is more likely to be severe in closely related species than in more distantly related forms, since at least a partial separation of niches is likely where morphological and behavioral adaptations diverge.

Ecologists who study interspecific competition in laboratory populations will be the first to point out that the experimental populations are living under conditions not at all like those in nature. Their experiments are specifically designed to single out and exaggerate one kind of regulatory process by controlling or eliminating other interactions that in nature may overrule or obscure the interaction being studied. Consequently, the difference in conditions needs to be carefully considered before it can be decided to what extent the laboratory data are applicable to the field. For one thing, the density is much higher in laboratory cultures than is usual in natural ecosystems; hence contacts between individuals are more frequent. If, in the case of the pair of *Tribolium* species, the ecosystems were "open" instead of "closed," and individuals of the dominant species were to immigrate (or be removed) at a considerable rate, the competition might be so reduced that both species could survive in the original culture. Or if the cultures were alternately placed in hot-wet and cool-dry conditions (to simulate seasonal weather changes) the advantage one species would have over the other might not continue for a long enough time for competition to run the full course to extinction of either species. One can think of many other complexities that might be realistic in nature. Are we then to assume that the culture experiments have no bearing on what happens under natural conditions?

To answer the question we should first point out that the laboratory ecosystem is well worth studying for its own sake, even if there were no direct applications to the larger problems of nature; just to be able to understand and predict what happens in the small ecosystem is justification enough for study. Actually, the study of laboratory populations does contribute to the understanding of natural populations, provided we also consider observations and experiments in the larger, more natural systems. Again, though, as we have emphasized a number of times, a multilevel approach is ultimately necessary, since study at each level of organization contributes something but not everything to the total picture (see Chapter 1). Most important, perhaps, laboratory work enables us to set up a tentative hypothesis of what could happen in nature. After the hypothesis has been tested experimentally and perhaps translated into a mathematical model we have something concrete to measure and test in a given natural situation.

For example, related species often replace one another rather abruptly in a natural gradient. The "*Tribolium* model," as shown in Table 6-2, would suggest that interspecific competition might explain such a distribution. We could test this hypothesis by removing one species and observing whether the adjacent species invades the vacated area. One investigator (Connell, 1961) working with barnacles in an intertidal gradient in Scotland did just such an experiment. In Scotland, as well as along the seacoast of northeastern North America, two species of barnacles are commonly found on the rocky shores, one species of genus *Chthamalus* occupying a band near the upper part of the intertidal zone and another, larger species of genus *Balanus* occupying a wide band below the *Chthamalus* population as shown diagrammatically in Fig. 6-4. Next time you take a walk along a rocky coast you can observe the zonal distribution of barnacles and other organisms for yourself. Although a zonal distribution might suggest competition, one could also explain it by assuming that physical factors in the gradient limit each species to a band quite independent of the other. In the study in Scotland, it was found that larvae of both species tended to settle over a wider range than occupied by the adult population (Fig. 6-4). When adult *Balanus* were cleared away and new ones kept from settling, the young *Chthamalus* survived and grew quite well in the upper part of the "*Balanus* zone" where they normally are not found. *Balanus*, however, did not extend into the

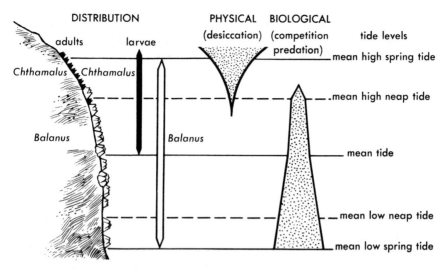

Fig. 6-4. Factors that control the distribution of two species of barnacles in an intertidal gradient. The young of each species settle over a wide range but survive to adulthood only within a more restricted range. Physical factors such as desiccation control upward limits of *Balanus* while biological factors such as competition and predation control downward distribution of *Chthamalus* in the lower portion of the intertidal gradient where physical environment is less limiting. This model can be considered to apply to more extensive gradients such as an arctic-to-tropics or a high-to-low altitude gradient. (Redrawn from J. H. Connell, *Ecology*, Vol. 142, 1961.)

"*Chthamalus* zone" even in the absence of *Chthamalus*. Fig. 6-4 summarizes the study, which also included consideration of predators and the effect of desiccation. It was noteworthy that biological regulation, including inter- and intraspecific competition and predation, proved to be important in the middle and lower part of the gradient, but not in the upper section where exposure to drying and temperature extremes limited the population to one species and relatively few individuals.

In another study an investigator (Pontin, *J. Animal Ecol.*, 30, 1961) poisoned colonies of one of two species of ants of the genus *Lasius* found living together in a field. The number of colonies of the remaining species increased the following year, indicating that competition was occurring even though the two species coexisted. In this case the niches of the two species are somewhat different; one species remains underground entirely, the other forages both underground and above ground. It was therefore presumed that competition was less severe than in the *Tribolium* model.

In still another study, this one involving fiddler crabs in an intertidal marsh, experiments demonstrated that interspecific competition was only one of several factors keeping two species separated (Teal, *Ecology*, 39, 1958). In this case one species responded more readily to a muddy substrate and the other to a sandy substrate; the sand-loving crab would invade the mud substrate if the other species was absent, but not too readily. It is probable that direct competition in the past played a part in the evolution of behavioral response to the substrate, which now plays the major role in keeping the species apart.

In addition to experimental evidence of the kind just cited there is a large body of observations that indicate that interspecific competition is generally important in nature, but less important, as indicated above, where climate, productivity, or other over-all ecosystem considerations are strongly limiting. Some of these general observations may be summarized as follows:

1. Closely related organisms often do not occur in the same place; or if they do, close study often shows that they use different energy sources, are active at different times of day or at different seasons, or otherwise occupy a different niche.

2. Where a large number of related species is present in a region, the niche of each is often narrower than when only a few species are present. Comparison of islands and mainlands often illustrates this trend. Thus, one investigator (Crowell, *Ecology,* 43, 1962) found that the cardinal was more abundant and occupied more marginal habitat in Bermuda, where the number of species of small birds (that is, potential competitors) was small, than on the United States mainland, where the cardinal is associated with a large number of other species.

3. Related species often replace one another in a gradient, as already mentioned.

In conclusion, we can say that what has come to be known in ecology as the *competition-exclusion principle,* or *Gause's principle* (after the Russian investigator who found that two species of *Paramecium* cannot live in the same culture), is one—but not the only—important biological regulation mechanism that results in either ecological separation of closely related species or reduction in density where species are able to coexist. However, one cannot conclude a priori from observed conditions in nature that competition is important, since "exclusion" from a given niche may be the result of other factors. Only the experimental approach can answer the question.

Predation

Although the energy flow of predators, that is secondary and tertiary consumers, is relatively small (see Fig. 3-2, p. 43), their role in regulating the primary consumers can be relatively great; in other words, a small number of predators can have a marked effect on the size of specific prey populations. On the other hand, as is also frequently the case, a predator may be only a minor factor in determining the size and growth rate of a prey population. As might be expected, there is a gradient of possibilities between these extreme situations. For the convenience of discussion let us consider three broad possibilities: (1) The predator is strongly limiting to the point of reducing the prey to extinction or near extinction. In the latter case violent oscillations in the size of the prey population will result, and, if the predator cannot turn to other populations for food, violent oscillations in predator numbers will also occur. (2) The predator can be regulatory in that it helps keep the prey population from outrunning its resources, or, put another way, it contributes to the maintenance of a steady state in the density of the prey. (3) The predator may be neither strongly limiting nor regulating.

Which situation exists for any pair of interacting species or groups of species depends on the *degree of vulnerability of the prey to the predator, as well as on the relative density levels and the energy flow from prey to predator.* From the predator's viewpoint this depends on how much energy it must expend to search for and capture the prey; from the prey's standpoint, this depends on how successfully individuals are able to avoid being eaten by the predator. A second principle about predator-prey interactions may be stated something as follows: *the limiting effects of predation tend to be reduced, and the regulating effects increased, where the interacting populations have had a common evolutionary history in a relatively stable ecosystem.* In other words, natural selection tends to reduce the detrimental effects of predation on both populations, since severe depression of a prey population by a predator can only lead to the extinction of one or both populations. Consequently, violent predator-prey interactions happen most frequently when the interaction is of recent origin (that is, when the two populations first become associated), or where there has been a recent large-scale disturbance in the ecosystem (as might be produced by man or by a climatic change).

Now that we have been so bold as to state two principles regarding predation, let us test them a bit and seek some examples. It is difficult for man to approach the subject of predation objectively. Although man himself is the greatest of all predators, often killing far beyond his needs, he tends to condemn all other predators without regard to the circumstance, especially if they prey on species he himself wishes to harvest. Sportsmen, among others, often have strong opinions against predators. The act of predation, such as a hawk catching a game bird, may be spectacular and easily observed whereas many other factors that may actually be more limiting to the bird population are not observed or are unknown to the untrained individual. For example, thirty years of objective study by Herbert L. Stoddard and his associates on the southwest Georgia game preserves have shown that hawks will not be a limiting factor to quail so long as vegetative escape cover lies near feeding areas so that birds can easily escape the attack of the hawk. Stoddard maintains high densities of quail by land management procedures that build up the food supply and refuge cover for the quail. In other words, his efforts are directed first toward improvement of the ecosystem specifically with the quail in mind. When this has been achieved, removal of hawks is unnecessary, even undesirable, because the quail are not vulnerable, and hawks also prey on rodents that eat quail eggs. Unfortunately, ecosystem management is more difficult and not so dramatic as shooting hawks. Game managers are often pressured into the latter even when they know better.

Now, let us cite an example of the opposite situation, where the predator exerts a marked effect. One of the author's students decided he could study a population of small rodents with more precision if he established a population on a small island in a new lake impoundment. Accordingly, he introduced a few pairs on the island, knowing that the animals could not leave it. For a while things went well; as the population grew, the student live-trapped and individually marked the animals and thus kept up with the births and deaths. Then, one day he went to the island to trap and found nothing. Investigation revealed a fresh mink den containing the bodies of many of his marked animals neatly cached away. Because the rodents were especially vulnerable on the island and could not escape or disperse, one mink had been able to find and kill them all!

To obtain an objective viewpoint it helps to think about predation from the population rather than from the individual standpoint. Predators, of course, are not beneficial to the individuals they kill, but they may be beneficial to the prey population as a whole. Some species of deer appear to be strongly regulated by predators. When the natural predators such as wolves, puma, bobcats, etc., are exterminated, man has found it difficult to control deer populations even though by hunting he himself becomes the predator. In the eastern United States man at first overhunted and exterminated the native deer from large areas. Then, there followed a period of hunting restriction and of reintroduction, and deer again became abundant. Now deer are more abundant in many places than under primeval conditions, with the result that they are overgrazing their forest habitat and even dying from starvation during the winter. The "deer problem" has become especially acute in such states as Michigan and Pennsylvania, where large areas of second-growth forest provide maximum food favoring an almost geometric increase that is often not checked by the level of hunting. Two points can be made here: (1) Some predation is necessary and beneficial in a population that has been adapted to it (and that lacks self-regulation); (2) When man removes the natural control mechanism, he must replace it with an equally efficient regulatory mechanism if severe oscillations are to be avoided. An inflexible bag limit set without regard to the density, available food, and habitat has generally failed to bring about the desired regulation. In agricultural areas, control of deer predators is of course necessary because of the possible damage they may do to domestic stock. But in wild regions, especially those not accessible to hunting, predators should be preserved for the good of the deer population, and for the good of the forest.

In Fig. 6-5 is shown a triangle of predatory interactions involving organisms that are not of direct economic importance to man; hence we should be able to consider these data without bias. For a number of years investigators at the University of Georgia Marine Institute at Sapelo Island have been studying the intertidal salt marsh as an ecosystem. The marsh is especially interesting to the ecologist because it is very productive yet contains only a limited number of species; hence interrelations between populations are more easily studied. In Chapter 4 (Fig. 4-4, p. 60) the mussel population of the marsh was used as an example of nutrient cycling. In the tall marsh grass growing along the salt creek banks live a small bird, the marsh wren, and a small rodent, the rice rat. Both feed on insects, snails, and, in the case of the rodent, small crabs and marsh grass. During the

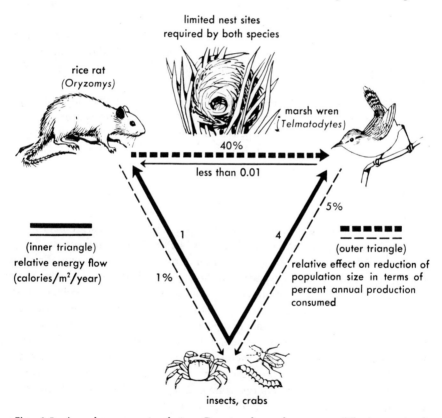

Fig. 6-5. A predator-prey triangle in a Georgia salt marsh ecosystem. The inner triangle shows estimated energy flow from prey to predator; the outer triangle is an estimate of the effect of predator on growth rate (production) of prey. Because the wren is vulnerable to the rice rat during the nesting season (when both species compete for nests in a limited habitat), the impact of predator on prey is not proportional to energy flow. See text for explanation. (Based on data of H. Sharp, H. Kale, and E. P. Odum.)

spring and summer the wren builds a globular nest out of grass in which to rear its young; during this season the rats prey on the eggs and young of the wren and often take over their nests for their own use. As shown in Fig. 6-5, the energy flow between invertebrates and the two vertebrates is small in terms of the large populations of the former. Thus the wren and the rat eat but a very small portion of their main food supply and, therefore, have little effect on the insect and crab populations; in this case predation is neither regulating nor controlling. In the annual cycle, wrens are a very minor food of the rat, yet because the wrens are especially vulnerable during the breeding season, the rat predation is a major factor in the wren mortality. When the density of rats was high, the wren population was depressed. Fortunately for the wrens, as yet undetermined factors limit the number of rats so that high density and resultant severe predation occur only in local areas.

We might consider the triangle between insects, rats, and wrens as a model for predation in general, since the triangular model shows how predation can be both a major and a minor item, depending on the relative density of predator and prey and the vulnerability of the prey to the predator. Remember, also, that the model does not mean that all bird-insect relationships are like this. The relationship depends on the species and the situation. Birds may be very effective predators on caterpillars that feed on leaf surfaces, and quite ineffective predators on leaf-mining insects that work inside the leaves.

Parasitism

Much of what has been said about predation also holds for parasitism. A population of parasites, whether they be bacteria, protozoans, fungi, helminth worms, or fleas, can be either strongly limiting, regulating, or relatively unimportant to a particular host population—in much the same manner as a predator may affect its prey. In fact, parasites and predators form a more or less continuous gradient ranging from tiny bacteria and viruses that live inside the host's tissues, to the large tigers of the ecosystem. The term "parasite" is usually used if the organism is small and actually lives in or on the host, which, therefore, is both energy source and habitat. In contrast, we think of a predator as being free living and larger than the prey, which serves as an energy source but not as habitat. All kinds of intermediate situations exist. The important point is that we are more interested in evaluating kinds of interactions than in classifying species into rigid categories. A given species may interact with other populations in more than one manner, depending on stage in the life cycle, locality, season, or other circumstance.

Although parasitism and predation are similar in terms of ecological regulation, important differences are found in the extremes of each situation. Parasitic organisms generally have higher reproductive rates and exhibit a greater "host" specificity than do most predators. Furthermore, they are often more specialized in structure, metabolism, and life history, as necessitated by their special internal environments and the problem of dispersal from one host to another. Some entire classes and orders of organisms, such as the Cestoda among the flatworms and the Sporozoa among the protozoans, have become adapted to parasitism. The most specialized species, such as the human malarial parasites, have a very complex life cycle that consists of a sequence of stages involving a succession of host tissues and an alternation of host species.

Host specificity of parasites is a very important consideration. Because many species of parasites can live only in one or a very few related species, the host-parasite interaction is especially intimate and potentially limiting to both populations. Man has often been able to utilize parasites in his attempt to regulate or control pests. In many cases insects that have been introduced from other parts of the world have been brought under control by transplanting the native parasites that regulated the insect in its original habitat; in other cases artificial propagation of parasites has helped. Practical biological control of this type is feasible with parasites that are specific for the species that man wishes to control. Such a parasite keeps constantly at work and can quickly adjust to increases and decreases in host numbers. In contrast, a pest can be rarely controlled by the introduction of a generalized predator that itself may become a pest if it spreads its attack to many other species. Thus, the English sparrow was introduced into New York City's Central Park for the purpose of controlling the elm spanworm. As we now know, this was a mistake; the sparrow not only did not control the insect (in the first place, tree caterpillars are not the main food item of this species) but it spread throughout the country and became a pest in many places. We have all heard about the introduction of the mongoose, a small, weasel-like predator, on islands; usually it was brought in for the purpose of controlling rats, but instead it often wreaks havoc with ground-nesting birds.

While we are on this subject we might as well point out that, contrary to popular opinion, domestic cats are not usually very effective in rat control. If rats are especially vulnerable by virtue of lack of shelter the cats may be effective, but usually this is not the case. Several years ago a very thorough study was made in the slum areas of Baltimore, where cats and rats were abundant. It was found that cats preferred to feed on garbage and were of little value in rat control. The most effective control was obtained by reducing the food and shelter used by rats.

In summary, predators are often important as regulators in the ecosystem as a whole; if somewhat specialized in their choice of prey (as in the puma-deer situation) they can also be effective at the population level, but usually not as effective as a parasite at this level. With insects, which are among man's most serious competitors, generalized predators such as insectivorous birds are very important in the forest as a whole since they provide constant inhibition to growth of all populations. However, if a particular species erupts, a specific parasite is much more effective. In well-regulated ecosystems there is an abundance of both generalized and specific controls. We have already commented on the "specialists" and the "generalists" of nature in Chapter 3.

The cardinal principle concerning the relation between severity of interaction and length of association mentioned in the previous section is especially applicable to parasitism. In many cases the most severe diseases of man and the plants and animals on which he depends are caused by organisms so recently acquired, or recently introduced, that the host has not developed protective immunity. The lesson for man, of course, is to avoid unnecessary introductions. Thus, the citizen should be patient when he crosses state and national boundaries and is asked to avoid transporting biological material that might contain a potential pest or disease.

Pest Control

At this point it would be well to consider from the ecological standpoint the general and often controversial subject of pest control. When man simplifies nature in order to obtain greater net production (as in agriculture) or to provide a comfortable environment for himself, some degree of chemical and mechanical control of competitors and pests often becomes necessary. The development of chemical pesticides has become an important science and industry that has resulted in much good for mankind. But as with any useful procedure it can be carried too far. Using a poison such as an insecticide, for example, in a corn field where biological control is often inadequate is one thing; broadcasting a chemical over forests or other complex ecosystems where its total effect is unknown is entirely another matter. In the latter situation the diverse natural mechanisms may be hampered more than the pest. The ecologist, therefore, might set up the following guide for both the specialist and layman: nonspecific poisons (those that may kill or interfere with a wide variety of life, including man) should be restricted to crops and other man-controlled and well-studied ecosystems, and should not (except as last resort) be used in the general environment or in complex natural ecosystems. Control measures that are as specific as possible for the pest in question should be used in the latter situations. A good example of a specific control is the successful use of x-ray sterilized males to control screw worm flies. In this case only the one species was affected, and all other natural predators and parasites were left to do their work.

Economic entomologists (specialists in insect control) point out that the present tendency to employ a "shot-gun" approach—that is, to broadcast insecticides over everything in the hope of hitting one small target without doing too much other damage—is only a temporary expediency to hold insects in check until more specific control methods can be developed. Unfortunately, the powerful weapons have had the tendency to lull us into complacency in our "war" with insects so that the ecological studies basic to pin-point control have lagged instead of being accelerated. A somewhat similar situation existed for a brief period in medicine when antibiotics were first overused in the same "shot-gun" manner; soon it became apparent that more harm than good could result from destruction of useful microorganisms in the body. The environmental "doctor" of the future must be at least as well-trained and wise as the medical doctor of today if the improvement in personal health is not to be canceled by a deterioration in public health.

Positive Interactions

So far we have been concerned with what might be called the negative interactions between individuals or populations; that is, interactions that result in inhibition to one or both parties. Positive interactions are equally important in the ecosystem. The wide acceptance of Darwin's theory of "survival of the fittest" directed special attention to such factors as competition as a means of bringing about natural selection. However, as Darwin himself pointed out, cooperation in nature is also important in natural selection. It seems reasonable to suppose that, like a balanced equation, negative and positive relations between populations eventually tend to balance if the ecosystem is to achieve any sort of stability.

We can think of positive interactions between populations of two or more species as taking three forms that, perhaps, represent an evolutionary series. *Commensalism* is a simple type of positive interaction in which one population benefits and the other is not affected to any measurable degree. A commensal relationship is especially common between sessile organisms and small motile organisms. The sea is a good place to observe such a relationship. Practically every worm burrow, shellfish, or sponge contains various "uninvited guests" that require the shelter or unused food of the host, but do neither harm nor good to the host. It is but a short step from this relation to parasitism on the one hand, or helpmate on the other. If two populations benefit each other, but are not essential to each other for survival, the relationship is often called *protocooperation;* if the association is necessary for the survival of both population, we designate the interaction by the term *mutualism*.

The late W. C. Allee studied and wrote extensively on the subject of protocooperation (see Suggested Reading List). He believed that the beginning of cooperation between species can be seen throughout the animal and plant kingdoms. Cooperation is thus not restricted to the human population. In the sea, for example, crabs and coelenterates often associate with mutual benefit even though the two species can live separately; the coelenterates grow on the backs of crabs, where they provide camouflage and protection (since these animals have stinging cells) for the crab. In return, the coelenterate is transported about and obtains particles of food when the crab captures and eats other animals.

Mutualism is extremely widespread and important. The mutualistic association of legumes and nitrogen-fixing bacteria has already been mentioned. Mutualism often involves species of very different taxonomic relationships. One whole group of plants, the lichens, are examples; in this case, algae and fungi are so closely associated that the botanist finds it convenient to consider the association as a single species. The lichen, in a sense, is a tiny ecosystem containing autotrophic (algae) and heterotrophic (fungi) components.

It is probable that protocooperation and mutualism can develop or evolve not only from commensalism but also from parasitism; as already hinted, parasites and hosts may become actually beneficial (from the population standpoint) after a long association. In some primitive lichens, for example, the fungi actually penetrate the algal cells, as shown in Fig. 6-6, and are thus essentially parasites of the algae. In the more advanced species the fungi mycelia do not break into the algal calls, but the two live in close harmony. (Fig. 6-6). So successful is the partnership that lichens are able to live in the harshest physical environments such as granite outcrops and arctic tundras.

In one sense mutualism is a model for a regulated ecosystem where

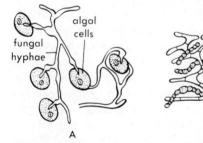
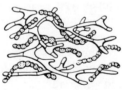
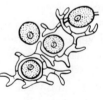

A	B	C
fungal hyphae actually penetrate into algal cells	fungal hyphae intermingle with algal filaments	fungal hyphae are closely appressed to algal cells but do not penetrate them

Fig. 6-6. A trend in evolution from parasitism to mutualism in the lichens. In some primitive lichens the fungi actually penetrate the algae cells, as in diagram A, whereas in more advanced species the two organisms live in greater harmony for mutual benefit, as in B and C.

even parasites and predators are useful in the sense that they "cooperate" for mutual survival. Man has made considerable progress in cooperation within his own population, and he is now also turning greater attention to achieving greater cooperation with other organisms for mutual benefit. There is much to be gained if we can transform negative interactions into positive ones. Again we come back to the theme with which this book began; that is, that man thrives best when he functions as a part of nature rather than as a separate unit that strives only to exploit nature for his immediate needs or temporary gain (as might a newly acquired parasite). Since man is a dependent heterotroph, he must learn to live in mutualism with nature; otherwise, like the "unwise" parasite, he may so exploit his "host" that he destroys himself.

The Special Problem of the Regulation of the Human Population

Much of the discussion in this chapter has a direct bearing on the human population situation. However, man differs from other organisms not only in his relatively greater power to control, but in his development of a complex culture that differs widely in different parts of the earth. Usually, culture is adaptive, but not infrequently cultural patterns of behavior persist long after they cease to be advantageous. A high birth rate, for example, is an advantage when density is low and resources unused, but not so advantageous when density is high and resources limited. The problem is so complex than a book at least as long as this one would be needed to develop the subject adequately. A number of thoughtful articles that introduce this vital subject are listed at the end of this chapter. Suffice it to say that most students of the human population feel that some form of self-regulation will be necessary eventually; hopefully, this regulation will come naturally through a change in cultural patterns. The alternatives, such as pestilence, severe pollution, war, and social stress, which might bring a halt to the human population explosion, are not pleasant to ponder. The productivity and carrying capacity of the biosphere for man can and certainly should be increased, but this only postpones the time when the human biomass must come into reasonable equilibrium with available space and food. In the meantime it would be safer if our population growth became more density dependent than is the case at the present time.

ECOLOGY AND EVOLUTION

So far in this chapter we have dealt with biological regulation as it occurs from day to day or over a short period of time (in terms of the geological time scale). Evolution of new varieties and species over long periods of time, of course, has been the means by which ecosystems have not only survived climatic changes but have achieved increasing biological diversity and increasing control over the physical environment. Since evolutionary processes are discussed fully in *Evolution* in this series, only an example or two need be cited here as a reminder that ecological processes such as competition, predation, succession, etc., go hand in hand with geological and genetic processes in shaping natural selection over the long term.

Especially interesting are the chromosomal patterns in wild populations of *Drosophila*, the fruit fly that has been the object of so much genetic research. Th. Dobzhansky and H. L. Carson, among others, report that in certain species of *Drosophila*, individuals from the central part of the range, where conditions are less limiting, exhibit considerable variability in the arrangement of genes on the paired chromosomes. Geneticists speak of this as heterozygosity for gene arrangement. In contrast, marginal populations, or those in active competition with closely related species, display more uniformity in chromosome structure (homozygosity for gene arrangement). In the latter situation the behavior and niche selection of the individual may be more restricted, but the possibilities for genetic recombinations are increased since exchange of genetic material between chromosome pairs is facilitated. Consequently, the opportunity for evolution of new ecotypes, races, or species by natural selection is increased. (See *Cold Spring Harbor Symposium Quantitative Biology*, Vol. 23, 1958.)

That ecological barriers can be as effective in speciation as are physical and geographical barriers has been well shown in a study by Keast (*Bull. Mus. Comp. Zool.*, Harvard Univ., Vol. 123, No. 8.) On the isolated continent of Australia almost as many species and varieties of birds have evolved as the result of ecological isolation as might have evolved had the continent been cut up into islands or otherwise subdivided by geographical barriers. For example, three tracts of rain forest that are separated by narrow strips of drier ecosystems along the eastern coast each have a different variety of the fig-parrot (*Opopsitta*). Ecological isolation in this case was as effective in speciation as geographical isolation.

SUGGESTED READING LIST

ALLEE, W. C., 1961. *Cooperation among animals with human implications.* New York: Henry Schuman. See also paperback edition, *Social life of animals,* Boston, Beacon Press, 1958.

ANDREWARTHA, H. G., 1961. *Introduction to the study of animal populations.* Chicago: University of Chicago Press.

BURKHOLDER, PAUL R., "Cooperation and conflict among primitive organisms," *American Scientist*, Vol. 40 (1952), pp. 601–631.

CALHOUN, JOHN B., "Population density and social pathology," *Scientific American*, February 1962, pp. 139–148.

COLE, LAMONT C., 1960. "Population dynamics," McGraw-Hill encyclopedia of science and technology, Vol. 10, p. 503.

DEEVEY, EDWARD S., "The probability of death," *Scientific American*, April 1950, pp. 58–60.

DICE, LEE R., 1952. *Natural communities*. Ann Arbor: University of Michigan Press. Chapters 10 to 14.

DUNBAR, M. J., "The evolution of stability in marine environments. Natural selection at the level of the ecosystem," *American Naturalist*, Vol. 94 (1960), pp. 129–136.

HUTNER, S. H., and MCLAUGHLIN, JOHN A., "Poisonous tides," *Scientific American*, August 1958, pp. 92–98.

HUXLEY, JULIAN, "World population," *Scientific American*, March 1956, pp. 64–76. See also Mentor paperback, *On population: three essays by Malthus, Huxley, and Osburn*.

KENDEIGH, S. CHARLES, 1961. *Animal ecology*. Englewood Cliffs, N.J.: Prentice Hall. Chapters 15 to 18 (population dynamics).

KNIPLING, E. F., "The eradication of the screw-worm fly," *Scientific American*, September 1960, pp. 54–61.

LACK, DAVID, 1954. *The natural regulation of animal numbers*. Oxford, England: Clarendon Press.

LAMB, I. MACKENZIE, "Lichens," *Scientific American*, October 1959, pp. 144–156.

MARGALEF, RAMON, "Succession of populations." In *The seas*. New York: Wiley. (In press.)

ODUM, EUGENE P., 1959. *Fundamentals of ecology*, 2d ed. Philadelphia: W. B. Saunders, pp. 257–270 (succession); Chapters 6 to 7 (populations).

OOSTING, H. J., 1956. *The study of plant communities*, 2d ed. San Francisco: Freeman. Chapter 10 (plant succession).

PARK, THOMAS, "Ecological experimentation with animal populations," *Scientific Monthly*, Vol. 81 (1955), pp. 271–275. (See also reference cited in Table 6-2.)

SWEETMAN, HARVEY L., 1960. *The principles of biological control*. Dubuque, Iowa: W. C. Brown.

WENT, FRITS, "The ecology of desert plants," *Scientific American*, April 1955, pp. 68–75.

CHAPTER SEVEN

MAJOR

ECOSYSTEMS

OF THE

WORLD
In the previous chapters examples from a variety of aquatic, terrestrial, and experimental ecosystems were selected to illustrate ecological principles that apply anywhere. As mentioned in Chapter 1, concentrating attention on one particular environment is also a useful approach since ecological factors and processes differ in relative importance in different environments. Pictorial models shown in Figs. 3-2 and 6-4, for example, brought out the fact that physical factors play the major role in controlling populations in some situations whereas biological factors (succession, competition, predations, etc.) may be more important in others. To consider species composition, productivity, limiting factors, and so on, as well as the impact of man in various parts of the biosphere would require a whole library of books; it is hoped that this brief chapter will encourage the student to further reading and a better appreciation of the reciprocal interactions of man and the landscape. The books and articles listed at the end of this chapter provide factual coverage, are thought provoking, and will help one appreciate what one sees during travel.

We would do well to start our world tour with the seas, the largest and most stable ecosystem. The sea presumably also was the first ecosystem, for life is now thought to have originated in the salt-water milieu.

THE SEAS

The major oceans (Atlantic, Pacific, Indian, Arctic, and Antarctic) and their connectors and extension cover approximately 70 percent of the earth's surface. Since there are likely to be phytoplankton under every square meter and since life in some form extends to the greatest depths, the seas are the largest and "thickest" of ecosystems. They are also biologically the most diverse. Marine organisms exhibit an incredible array of adaptations, ranging from floating devices that keep the tiny plants within the upper layers of water, to the huge mouths and stomachs of deep-sea fish that live in a dark, cold world where meals are bulky but few and far between. As shown in Fig. 3-3, the continental shelf areas are fairly productive especially where upwelling occurs; sea food harvested here is an important source of protein and minerals for man. The vast stretches of the deep sea, however, are mostly semidesert with considerable total energy flow (because of the large area) but not much per unit of area. The autotrophic layer (photic zone) is so small in comparison with the heterotrophic layer that the nutrient supply in the former is limiting (see Chapter 3). Even if man is not able to obtain much food from the deep-sea area it is nevertheless very important to him, for the seas act as a giant regulator that helps to moderate land climates and maintain favorable concentrations of carbon dioxide and oxygen in the atmosphere. The deep sea is also a reservoir of valuable minerals lost from the continents.

Physical factors dominate life in the ocean (Fig. 7-1). Waves, tides, currents, salinities, temperatures, pressures, and light intensities largely deter-

Fig. 7-1. The seas. The never-ending wave motion seen in the photograph serves to emphasize the dominance of physical factors in the open ocean. (Courtesy Woods Hole Oceanographic Institute and D. M. Owen.)

mine the makeup of biological communities that, in turn, have considerable influence on the composition of bottom sediments and gases in solution. The food chains of the sea begin with the smallest known autotrophs and end with the largest of animals (giant fish, squid, and whales). The study of the physics, chemistry, geology, and biology of the sea are combined into a sort of "superscience" called oceanography, which is becoming increasingly important as an international force. Although exploration of the sea is not quite as expensive as exploration of outer space, a considerable outlay of ships, shore laboratories, equipment, and specialists are needed. Most research is now carried out by a relatively few large institutions backed by government subsidies. Despite the considerable work that has been done, the sea still contains enough mysteries to challenge mankind for a long time to come. One mystery now perhaps about to be solved involves the "deep scattering layer," a phantom barrier or false bottom that reflects the sonic waves of ship echo-sounders. The layer is apparently composed of organisms, but just what kind is not yet known.

ESTUARIES AND SEASHORES

Between the seas and the continents lie a band of diverse ecosystems that are not just transition zones but have ecological characteristics of their own. Whereas physical factors such as salinity and temperature are much more variable near shore than in the sea itself, food conditions are so much better that the region is packed with life. Along the shore live thousands of adapted species that are not to be found in the open sea, on land, or in fresh water. A rocky shore, a sand beach, an intertidal mud flat, and a tidal estuary dominated by salt marshes are shown in Fig. 7-2 to illustrate four kinds of marine inshore ecosystems. The word "estuary" (from Latin *aestus,* tide) refers to a river mouth or coastal bay where the salinity is intermediate between the sea and fresh water, and where tidal action is an important physical regulator.

Estuaries and inshore marine waters are among the most naturally fertile in the world (see Fig. 3-3). There are at least five mechanisms and conditions that maintain biological energy flow at rates often considerably greater than those in the adjacent sea or fresh water: (1) Tidal action promotes a rapid circulation of nutrients and food, and aids in the rapid removal of the waste products of metabolism. (2) A diversity of plant species and life forms provides a continuous photosynthetic carpet despite variable physical conditions. The three major life forms of autotrophs that work together to maintain a high gross production rate are: (a) phytoplankton; (b) benthic microflora—algae living in and on mud, sand, rocks, or other hard surfaces, and bodies or shells of animals; (c) large attached plants—the seaweeds, submerged eel grasses, and emergent marsh grasses. (3) An estuary is often an efficient nutrient trap that is partly physical (differences in salinities cause vertical as well as horizonal mixing of water masses) and partly biological, as was illustrated by the example of the mussel population (Fig. 4-4). (4) A year-round primary production by a succession of "crops," even in northern regions. (5) Close contact between autotrophic and heterotrophic layers (see Chapter 3).

Organisms have evolved many adaptations to cope with tidal cycles, thereby enabling them to exploit the many advantages of living in an estuary. Some animals, such as fiddler crabs, have internal "biological clocks" that help to time their feeding activities to the most favorable part of the tidal cycle. If such animals are experimentally removed to a constant environment they continue to exhibit rhythmic activity synchronous with the tides.

As the late Aldo Leopold, a great American conservationist, has said (see references at the end of this chapter), man has difficulty in understanding organic function in any system he has not built himself. Hence, he will permit destructive tampering with the landscape by the rankest amateurs even though he would not permit an amateur to tinker with his expensive watch. The average layman seldom appreciates the useful but complex biological interrelations and fluid mechanics of estuaries. An often underestimated value of biological structures along shore such as dune grasses, oyster reefs, and marsh grasses lies in their protection against storms. Converting already useful estuaries into open sewers for industrial wastes, or into corn fields or house sites for which the topography is not well suited, is not in the best interest of man. Conservationists and trained marine en-

---

Fig. 7-2. (*See the two following pages.*) Four types of coastal ecosystems. A: A rocky shore on the California coast, characterized by underwater seaweed beds, tidepools with colorful invertebrates, sea lions ("seals") and sea birds (seen in the water and on rocks off shore). B: A sand beach with ghost crab near its burrow. C: An intertidal mud flat in Massachusetts, during low tide. Although mud flats may look like deserts on the surface they can, when not polluted or overexploited by man, support very large populations of shellfish and other animals. Shown in the picture is Dr. Paul Galtsoff, a life-long student of marine animals, with some 30-odd clams dug from a single square foot (to depth of 8 inches) of mud flat. Animals of mud flats are of two general feeding types: filter feeders such as the clams, which filter out food particles from water, and deposit feeders such as many gastropods that ingest the "mud" from which organic matter is extracted in the intestine. Part of the food that supports the dense populations is produced by algae living on and in the mud, and part is brought in by each tide. D: A productive tidal estuary on the coast of Georgia, showing sounds, networks of tidal creeks, and vast areas of salt marsh. The shallow creeks and marshes not only support an abundance of stationary organisms but they also serve as nursery grounds for shrimp and fish that later move off shore where they are harvested by trawlers. (A, B, and C, U. S. Department of Interior, Fish and Wildlife Service. D, University of Georgia Marine Institute.)

Fig. 7-2A

Fig. 7-2B

Fig. 7-2C

Fig. 7-2D

vironmental engineers have recently become alarmed by the needless destruction of coastal resources. Ultimately it may be necessary to set up some kind of zoning or conservation district plan so that the use of such areas by man can be placed on a sound ecological basis.

STREAMS AND RIVERS

The history of man has often been shaped by the rivers that provide water, transportation, and a means of waste disposal. Although the total surface area of rivers and streams is small compared to that of oceans and land mass, rivers are among the most intensely used by man of natural ecosystems. As in the case of estuaries, the need for "multiple use" (as contrasted to a "single use" approach to such ecosystems as cropland) demands that the various areas (water supply, waste disposal, fish production, flood control, etc.) be considered together and not as entirely separate problems.

From the energetic standpoint rivers and streams are incomplete ecosystems; that is, some portion, often a large portion, of the energy flow is based on organic matter imported from adjacent terrestrial ecosystems (or sometimes from adjacent lakes). How best to determine the import rate is a problem ecologists have not yet solved. Since streams are naturally adapted to organic matter they make ideal disposal systems for organic wastes, provided the load is not too great. Some of the ecological principles relating to stream pollution have already been discussed (Chapter 5). Suffice it to say here that oxygen and suspended matter are two factors that often become critical.

The stream ecologist finds it convenient to consider flowing-water ecosystems under two subdivisions: (1) streams in which the basin is eroding and the bottom, therefore, is generally firm, and (2) streams in which material is being deposited and, therefore, the bottom is generally composed of soft sediments. In many cases these situations alternate in the same stream, as may be seen in the "rapids" and "pools" of small streams. Aquatic communities are quite different in the two situations owing to the rather different conditions of existence. The communities of pools resemble those of ponds in that a considerable development of phytoplankton may occur and the species of fish and aquatic insects are the same or similar to those found in ponds and lakes. The life of the hard-bottom rapids, however, is composed of more unique and specialized forms, such as the net-spinning caddis (larvae of insects called caddis flies or Trichoptera), which constructs a fine silk net that removes food particles from the flowing waters.

A tremendous volume of water is cycled between nature and highly industrialized society; only a very small part of it is used for man's physiological needs. So rapid is the turnover in many places that the resident time in nature is not long enough to allow detergents and other resistant wastes to decompose completely before the water again reaches the faucet. So critical are water problems that the federal government has recently moved to establish a series of regional water research laboratories where water chemists, environmental engineers, and aquatic ecologists can work together.

LAKES AND PONDS

In the geological sense, most basins that now contain standing fresh water are relatively young. The life span of ponds ranges from a few weeks or months in the case of small seasonal ponds to several hundred years for larger ponds. Although a few lakes, such as Lake Baikal in Russia, are ancient, most large lakes date only as far back as the ice ages. Standing water ecosystems may be expected to change with time at rates more or less inversely proportional to size. Although geographical discontinuity of fresh waters favors speciation, the lack of isolation in time does not. Generally speaking, the species diversity is low in fresh-water communities and many taxa (species, genera, families) are widely distributed within a continential mass and even between adjacent continents. For this reason, and because standing-water bodies are relatively self-contained from the energetic standpoint, a pond was considered in some detail in Chapter 2 as an example of an ecosystem.

Distinct zonation and stratification are characteristic features of lakes and large ponds. Typically, one may distinguish a *littoral zone* containing rooted vegetation along shore, a *limnetic* zone of open water dominated by plankton, and a deep-water profundal zone containing only heterotrophs. In temperate regions, lakes often become thermally stratified during summer and again in winter, owing to differential heating and cooling. The upper part of the lake, or *epilimnion* (from Greek *limnion*, lake), becomes temporarily isolated from the lower water, or *hypolimnion*, by a *thermocline* zone that acts as a barrier to exchange of materials. Consequently, the supply of oxygen in the hypolimnion and nutrients in the epilimnion may run short. During spring and fall, as the entire body of water approaches the same temperature, mixing again occurs. "Blooms" of phytoplankton often follow this seasonal rejuvenation of the ecosystem.

Primary production in standing-water ecosystems depends on the chemical nature of the basin, the nature of imports from streams or land, and the depth. Shallow lakes are usually more fertile than deep ones for reasons already outlined in the discussion of the seas (see Chapter 3 and Fig. 3-3). For example, one investigator (Rawson, *Ecology*, 33:513) found that the pounds of fish commercially harvested per acre of surface in a series of large Canadian lakes was inversely proportional to the mean depth. Lakes are

A

B

C

often classified into *oligotrophic* ("few foods") and *eutrophic* ("good foods") types depending on their productivity. What has now come to be known as "artificial eutrophication" of lakes has created difficult problems in the vicinity of metropolitan areas and crowded summer resorts. Inorganic fertilizers of sewage effluent entering lakes increases their primary production rates and perhaps also the fish production, but the composition of the aquatic community may change in ways that are not popular with the public. For example, game fish such as trout, which require cool, clear, oxygen-rich waters, may disappear; growth of algae and other aquatic plants may become so great as to interfere with swimming, boating, and sport fishing; or undecomposed dissolved organics may impart a bad taste to water even after it has passed through water purification systems. Thus, a biologically poor lake may be preferable to a fertile one from the standpoint of water use and recreation. Again, we have a paradox. In some parts of the biosphere man is doing everything possible to increase its fertility in order to feed himself, whereas in other places he does everything possible to prevent fertility (by removing nutrients, poisoning plants, etc.) in order to maintain a pleasant environment.

Constructing artificial ponds and lakes (impoundments) is one of the conspicuous ways in which man has changed the landscape in regions that lack natural bodies of water. In the United States almost every farm now has at least one farm pond; large impoundments have been constructed on practically every river. Most of this activity works to the benefit of both man and the landscape, for water and nutrient cycles are stabilized and the added diversity is a welcome change in man's usual tendency to create a monotonous landscape. However, the impoundment idea can be carried too far; covering up fertile land with a body of water that cannot yield much food may not be the best land use.

People seem strangely unprepared for the changes that arise from ecological succession in artificial ponds and lakes. Somehow, once a lake has been created it is expected to remain the same as would a skyscraper or bridge. Instead, of course, all the biological processes of succession that were described in Chapter 6 (see Table 6-1) take place, not to mention changes due to the erosion in the often poorly protected watershed. The in-

---

Fig. 7-3. *(Facing).* Three fresh-water ecosystems. A: A fresh-water marsh in the Sacramento National Wildlife Refuge in California, where flocks of geese find refuge and shelter in productive aquatic and semiaquatic vegetation. B: A natural pond in the grassland region of Western Canada. C: Convergence of two streams in northern New Jersey. The stream in the foreground flows from a watershed protected by grass and trees; the stream entering from the left is badly polluted with silt as a result of poor agriculture. (A and B, U. S. Department of Interior, Fish and Wildlife Service. C, U. S. Soil Conservation Service.)

crease in species diversity and decrease in net community production often lead to poor fish as the pond ages. A simple solution (but not always the desirable or practical one) is to drain the pond periodically and start over so that body of water is maintained in a young or early successional stage. Such "fallowing" of ponds has been practiced for centuries in Europe and in the Orient.

Since shallow bodies of water can be as productive as an equal area of land, *aquaculture* can be a useful supplement to agriculture, especially where tillable land is scarce. Aquaculture is a highly developed art and science in countries such as Japan, where large yields of algae, fish, and shellfish are obtained from managed but seminatural bodies of both fresh and salt water. The approach to fish culture, interestingly enough, is greatly influenced by population density. Where man is crowded and hungry, ponds are managed for their yields of herbivores such as carp; yields of 1000 to 5000 pounds per acre per year can be obtained. Where man is not crowded or hungry, sport fish are what is desired; since these fish are usually carnivores produced at the end of long food chains, the yields are much less, 100 to 500 pounds per acre per year.

FRESH-WATER MARSHES

Much of what was said about estuaries also applies to fresh-water marshes (Fig. 7-3A); they tend to be naturally fertile ecosystems. Tidal action, of course, is absent, but periodic fluctuation in water levels resulting from seasonal and annual rainfall variations often accomplishes the same thing in terms of maintaining long-range stability and fertility. Fires during dry periods deepen the water-holding basins and also aid the decomposition of accumulated organic matter. In fact, if such events do not occur, the build-up of sediments and peat (undecayed organic matter), which occurs in ecological succession, tends to lead to the invasion of terrestrial woody vegetation. Where man controls water levels by dikes in marshes he generally finds that chemical herbicides or mechanical methods have to be used if the area is to continue to exist as a true fresh-water marsh ecosystem suitable for ducks and other semiaquatic organisms.

The general public prejudice against marshes is understandable, since they are sometimes the home of mosquitoes and other disease carriers and pests. Before much was known about the life history and ecology of the arthropods and snails as disease carriers, destroying their habitat (that is, draining the marsh) was about the only solution. Our present knowledge now makes it unnecessary to destroy the ecosystem in order to control undesirable species.

In addition to producing ducks and fur-bearers, marshes are valuable in maintaining water tables in adjacent ecosystems. The Florida Everglades are an exceptionally large and interesting stretch of fresh-water marshes characterized by naturally fluctuating water levels. Complete drainage (even if possible or otherwise desirable) would not only ruin the area as a wildlife paradise but would also be risky in that salt water might then intrude into the underground water supply needed by the large coastal cities.

Finally, it is significant that rice culture, one of the most productive and dependable of agricultural systems yet devised by man, is actually a type of fresh-water marsh ecosystem. The flooding, draining, and careful rebuilding of the rice paddy each year has much to do with the maintenance of continuous fertility and high production of the rice plant, which, itself, is a kind of cultivated marsh grass.

DESERTS

Desert ecosystems occur in regions with less than 10 inches of annual rainfall, or sometimes in hot regions where there is more rainfall but unevenly distributed in the annual cycle. Lack of rain in the mid-latitudes is often due to stable high-pressure zones; deserts in temperate regions often lie in "rain shadows," that is, where high mountains block off moisture from the seas. Two types of North American deserts are shown in Fig. 7-4, a "cool" desert in Washington, with sagebrush, and a "hot" desert in Arizona, where creosote bushes and cacti are conspicuous. The characteristic spacing of desert vegetation and the possibility of "birth control" mechanisms were discussed in Chapter 6. Four very distinctive life forms of plants are adapted to the desert ecosystem: (1) The annuals (such as cheat grass, shown in Fig. 7-4B), which avoid drought by growing only when there is adequate moisture (see Chapter 4, p. 73). (2) The desert shrub with numerous branches arising from a short basal trunk, and small, thick leaves that may be shed during dry periods; the desert shrub survives by its ability to become dormant before wilting occurs. (3) The succulents, such as the cacti of the New World or the euphorbias of the Old World, which store water in their tissues. (4) Microflora, such as mosses, lichens, and blue-green algae that remain dormant in the soil but are able to respond quickly to cool or wet periods.

Animals such as reptiles and some insects are "preadapted" to deserts, for their impervious integuments and dry excretions enable them to get along on the small amount of water produced in the body as a result of the breakdown of carbohydrates. Mammals as a group are poorly adapted to deserts but some few species have become secondarily adapted. A few species of nocturnal rodents, for example, that excrete very concentrated urine and do not use water for temperature regulation, can live in the desert without drink-

A

B

Fig. 7-4. Two types of deserts in western North America. A: A "hot" desert in Arizona. B: A "cool" desert in eastern Washington in early spring. The desert shrub life form is illustrated by the dark creosote bushes in (A) and the sagebrush in (B). Note the rather even spacing of shrubs, especially evident in the upper picture. The succulent life form is represented by cacti in (A) and the desert annual is represented by the cheat grass growing between the sage bushes in (B). The objective of the radioactive tracer experiment shown in (B) was to determine the relative uptake from soil of specific minerals by the two life forms growing within the metal ring. (A, courtesy Dr. R. R. Humphries. B, Hanford Atomic Products Operation.)

ing water. Other animals such as camels must drink but are able to store water in their bodies.

Where water is limiting but soils themselves are not, irrigation can convert deserts into some of our most productive agricultural land. Whether productivity continues or is only a temporary "bloom" depends on how well man is able to stabilize biogeochemical cycles and energy flow at the new, increased rates. As the large volume of water passes through the irrigation system, salts may be left behind that will gradually accumulate over the years until they become limiting, unless means of avoiding this difficulty are devised. The water supply itself can fail if the watershed from which it comes is abused. The ruins of old irrigation systems, and the civilizations they supported, in the deserts of the Old World warn that the desert does not continue to bloom for man unless he understands the laws of the ecosystem and acts accordingly.

TUNDRAS

Between the forests to the south and the Arctic ocean and polar icecaps to the north lies a circumpolar band of about 5 million acres of treeless country called the arctic tundra (Fig. 7-5). Smaller, but ecologically similar, regions found above the tree limit on high mountains are called alpine tundras. As in deserts, a master physical factor rules these lands, but it is heat rather than water that is in short supply in terms of biological function. Precipitation is also low, but water as such is not limiting because of the very low evaporation rate. Thus, we might think of the tundra as an arctic desert, but it can best be described as a wet arctic grassland that is frozen for a large portion of the year.

Although the tundras are often known as the "barren grounds" and may be expected to have a relatively low biological diversity, a surprisingly large number of species have evolved remarkable adaptations to survive the cold. The thin vegetation mantle is composed of lichens, grasses, and sedges, which are among the hardiest of land plants. During the long daylight hours (long photoperiod) of the brief summer the primary production rate is remarkably good where topographic conditions are favorable (as in low-lying areas of Fig. 7-5B). The thousands of shallow ponds, as well as the adjacent Arctic ocean, provide additional food to tundra food chains. There is enough combined aquatic and terrestrial net production, in fact, to support not only thousands of breeding migratory birds and emerging insects during the summer, but also permanent resident mammals that remain active throughout the year. The latter range from large animals such as musk ox, caribou, reindeer (Fig. 7-5A), polar bears, wolves, and marine mammals, to lemmings that tunnel about in the vegetation mantle. The large land heribivores are

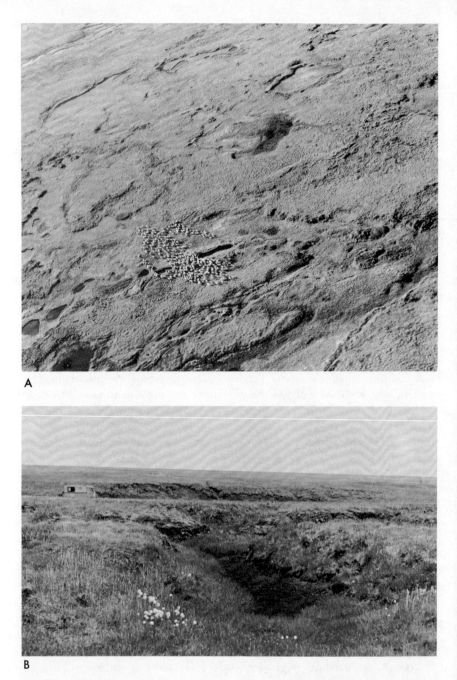

A

B

Fig. 7-5. The tundra. A: Aerial view of tundra, showing herd of reindeer. The bumpy nature of the landscape is due to frost action; note, also, numerous small ponds. B: Close-up of tundra in August near the Arctic Research Laboratory at Point Barrow, Alaska, showing grass and sedge vegetation. (A, U. S. Department of Interior, Fish and Wildlife Service. B, courtesy R. E. Shanks and John Koranda.)

highly migratory, since there is not enough net production in any one local area to support them. The dramatic ups and downs in the density of lemmings, and the general instability of tundra populations were discussed in Chapter 6. The difference in response to light by plants in the arctic and alpine tundras was mentioned in Chapter 5 (Fig. 5-1).

Ecologists have recently shown a heightened interest in studying the tundra, not only because some parts of it are being increasingly used by man, but because its simplified biological structure provides a favorable site for basic studies of the ecosystem.

GRASSLANDS

Natural grasslands occur where rainfall is intermediate between that of desert lands and forest lands. In the temperate zone this generally means an annual precipitation between 10 and 30 inches, depending on temperature, seasonal distribution of the rainfall, and the water-holding capacity of the soil. Tropical grasslands may receive up to 60 inches concentrated in a wet season that alternates with a prolonged dry season. Grasslands are one of the most important of terrestrial ecosystem types; large areas occupy the interior of the principal continents. About one third of the United States is grassland, the rest being mostly forest land and a relatively small total area of true desert, marsh, estuaries, and alpine tundras.

Several aspects of North American grasslands are shown in Fig. 7-6. Dominant plant-life forms are the grasses, which range from tall species (5 to 8 feet) to short ones (6 inches or less) that may be bunch grass types (growing in clumps) or sod formers (with underground rhizomes). A well-developed grassland community contains species with different temperature adaptations, one group growing in the cool part of the season (spring and fall) and another in the hot part (summer); the grassland as a whole "compensates" for temperature, thus extending the period of primary production (see Chapter 5). Forbs (nongrassy herbs) are often important components, and woody plants (trees and shrubs) also occur in grasslands either as scattered individuals (producing what is often called a "savanna") or in belts or groups along streams and rivers.

The grassland community builds an entirely different type of soil as compared to a forest, even when both start with the same parent mineral material. Since grass plants are short lived as compared to trees, a large amount of organic matter is added to the soil. The first phase of decay is rapid, resulting in little litter but much humus; in other words, humification is rapid but mineralization is slow. Consequently, grassland soils may contain 5 to 10 times as much humus as forest soils. The dark grassland soils are among those best suited for growing man's principal food plants such

A

B

C

D

Fig. 7-6. *(Above and facing.)* Four aspects of grasslands. A: Natural grassland with herd of bison on the National Bison Range in Montana. B: Cattle grazing in natural grassland that is in good condition. C: Overgrazed grassland that has the appearance of a man-made desert. D: Grassland converted to intensive grain farming. (A and D, U. S. Department of Interior, Fish and Wildlife Service. B and C, U. S. Forest Service.)

---

as corn and wheat (Fig. 7-6D), which, of course, are species of cultivated grasses.

The role of fire in maintaining grassland vegetation in competition with woody vegetation in warm or moist regions was discussed in Chapter 5 (see Fig. 5-5), and the characteristic, although relatively brief, pattern of ecological succession in grasslands was described in Chapter 6.

Large herbivores are a characteristic feature of grasslands (Fig. 7-6A). These are mostly large mammals, but large grazing birds are known to have occurred in the original fauna of New Zealand. The "ecological equivalence" of bison, antelope, and kangaroos in grasslands of different geographical regions was mentioned in Chapter 2. The large grazers come in two "life forms": running types, such as those mentioned above, and burrowing types, such as ground squirrels and gophers. When man uses grasslands as natural pastures he usually replaces the native grazers with his domestic kind—that is, cattle, sheep, and goats. Since grasslands are adapted to heavy energy flow along the grazing food chain, such a switch is ecologically sound. However, man has had a persistent history of misuse of grassland resources by virtue of allowing overgrazing (Fig. 7-6C) and overplowing. The result is that many grasslands are now man-made deserts. The importance of ecological indicators in the early detection of overgrazing was mentioned in Chapter 5.

What to do about the African grasslands that contain an unusual diversity of mammalian grazers is a question now facing the emerging nations of that area as they strive to raise nutritional levels in the human population. Many ecologists believe that it would be better to harvest the antelope, hippopotamuses, and wildebeests on a sustained-yield basis rather than exterminate them in order to substitute cattle. For one thing, the natural diversity means broader use of primary production. Further, the native species are immune to the many tropical parasites and diseases to which cattle are vulnerable.

FORESTS

In Chapter 3 (Fig. 3-2) and again in Chapter 6 (p. 86) the point was made that the open sea and the forest are, in a comparative sense, the extreme ecosystem types in the biosphere in regard to standing crop biomass and the relative importance of physical and biological regulation. As shown in Fig. 6-2, well-ordered and often lengthy ecological succession is characteristic with herbaceous plants often preparing the way for trees. Consequently, in any one forest region one may see a variety of vegetations that represent stages in succession as well as adaptations to varying soil and moisture conditions of the substrate. Because the range of temperatures that will allow forest development is extremely wide, a sequence of forest types replace one another in a north-south gradient. Moisture is more critical to the tree life form, but forests occupy a fairly wide gradient from dry to extremely wet situations.

Fig. 7-7 shows three distinctly different forests in a north-south gradient. The northernmost forests, which form a belt just south of the tundra, are characterized by evergreen conifers of the genera *Picea* (spruce) and *Abies* (fir); species diversity is low, often with one or two species of trees forming pure stands. Deciduous forests are characteristic of the more southern moist-temperate regions; these forest have more pronounced stratification and a greater species diversity. Pines (*Pinus*) are found in both northern coniferous and temperate deciduous forest regions, often as seral stages. The third type, the tropical forests, range from broad-leaved evergreen rain forests, where rainfall is abundant and distributed throughout the annual cycle, to tropical deciduous forests that lose their leaves during a dry season. Two life-forms, the vine (lianas) and the epiphyte (air plants), are especially characteristic of tropical forests; a few species of these life forms are found in northern

Fig. 7-7. Three forest types in a north-south temperature gradient. A: Northern coniferous forest of spruce in Idaho. B: Temperate deciduous forest of oaks, hickories, and other hardwoods in Indiana. C: A tropical rain forest in Puerto Rico. (A and B, U. S. Forest Service. C, courtesy University of Puerto Rico.)

forests, but only in the tropical regions do they make up a conspicuous portion of the biological structure. Species diversity reaches a maximum in tropical rain forests; there may be more species of plants and insects in a few acres of tropical rain forests than in the entire flora and fauna of Europe.

Two forest types in what might be thought of as a moisture gradient are shown in Fig. 7-8. The chaparral woodland is a "fire type" in that it is naturally subjected to fires and is adapted to this factor (see p. 73). The moist-temperate rain forests, such as those along the coasts from northern California to Washington, do not have as great a species diversity as tropical forests, but individual trees and the total timber volume may be greater.

A good place in which to observe the pattern of forests in relation to climate and substrate is the Great Smoky Mountain National Park located along the Tennessee-North Carolina border. Fig. 7-9 is a diagram that will help one view the landscape with the eyes of the ecologist. The altitude change produces a north-south temperature gradient, whereas the valley and ridge topography provides a gradient of soil moisture conditions at any given altitude. At sea level one would have to travel many hundreds of miles to observe the variety of climates present in a small geographical area in the Smokies. The pattern of vegetation along the gradients stands out best in May and early June (when floral displays are also spectacular), but the remarkable way in which forests adapt to topography and climate is evident at any time of year.

As shown in Fig. 7-9, the forests of the Smokies range from open oak and southern pine stands on the drier, warmer slopes at low altitudes, to northern coniferous forests of spruce and fir on the cold, moist summits. The southern pine stands extend upward along the exposed ridges, and the northern hemlock forest extends downward in the protected ravines where moisture and local temperature conditions are those of higher altitudes. The maximum diversity of tree species occurs in sheltered (that is, moist) locations about mid-way in the temperature gradient.

The reason why some of the high, exposed slopes of the Smokies are covered with rhododendron thickets or grass instead of trees has not been adequately explained. These "balds" are not alpine tundras, for the altitude is not great enough for a true treeless zone. Whatever the reason (perhaps fire) for their original establishment, the shrub community is now so well established that it resists invasion by the forest. In this situation one can observe how whole communities, as well as the individuals in them, compete with one another. The eventual outcome may depend on the occurrence of some event such as fire or storms that might tip the balance in favor of one or the other ecological system.

Timber production and the practice of forestry pass through two phases. The first phase involves the harvest of net production that has been stored as wood over a period of years. When the accumulated growth of the past

A

B

Fig. 7-8. Two forests adjusted to different moisture and fire conditions. A: Chaparral woodland, a dwarf forest of the winter rain–summer drought climate of coastal California; periodic fires are a major environmental factor. B: A douglas fir stand in Washington, one of several forest types in the moist Pacific Northwest that develop some of the largest volumes of timber in the world. (U. S. Forest Service.)

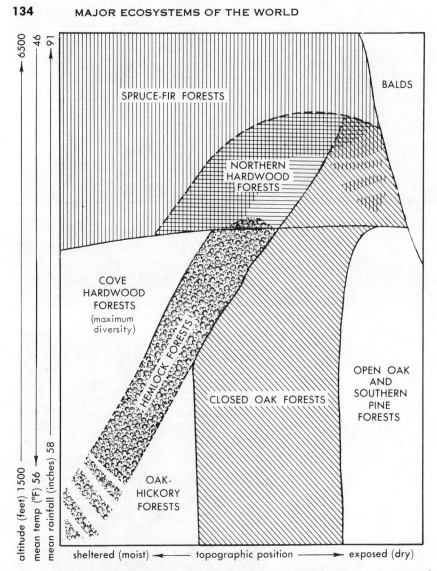

Fig. 7-9. The pattern of forest vegetation in the Great Smoky Mountain National Park as related to temperature and moisture gradients. See text for explanation. (Diagram prepared by R. Shanks after R. H. Whittaker, *Ecological Monographs,* 1952.)

has been used up, man must adjust his forestry practice to harvesting no more than the annual growth if he expects to have any wood products at all. In the northwestern United States the first phase is still underway; the annual timber cut in this region is about double the annual growth. In contrast, the second phase has been reached in the southeastern United States. Most of the old timber has been cut; hence forestry practice is primarily concerned with young forests where the harvest now balances annual growth. Although, as pointed out in Chapter 6, the annual net production in a young forest is often greater than that of an old forest, the quality of the wood for lumber use is not as good, since wood of fast-growing young trees is not as dense as that of slow-growing older trees. As in so many situations, some compromise between quantity and quality should be the ultimate goal of applied science.

Human civilization has so far reached its greatest development in what was originally forest and grassland in temperate regions. Consequently, most temperate forests and grasslands have been greatly modified from their primeval condition, but the basic nature of these ecosystems has by no means been changed. Man, in fact, tends to combine features of both grasslands and forests into a habitat for himself that might be called *forest edge*. When man settles in grassland regions he plants trees around his homes, towns, and farms, so that small patches of forest become dispersed in what may have been treeless country. Likewise, when man settles in the forest he replaces most of it with grasslands and croplands, but leaves patches of the original forest on farms and around residential areas. Many of the smaller plants and animals originally found in both forest and grassland are able to adapt and thrive in close association with man and his domestic or cultivated species. The American robin, for example, once a bird of the forest, has become so well adapted to the man-made forest edge that it has not only increased in numbers but has also extended its geographical range. Most native species that persist in regions heavily settled by man become useful members of the forest-edge ecosystem of man, but a few become pests. The worst pests, however, are more likely to be species introduced from afar, as was discussed in Chapter 6.

If we consider croplands and pastures as modified grassland of early successional types, then man depends on grasslands for food, but likes to live and play in the shelter of the forest. At the risk of oversimplifying the situation we might say that man in common with other heterotrophs seeks two basic things from the landscape: "production" and "protection." But unlike lower organisms, he also finds esthetic enjoyment in the beauty of natural landscapes. For mankind, forests provide all three needs, but especially the latter two. In many cases the monetary value of the wood, if harvested all at once, is far less than the value of the intact forest that provides recreation, watershed protection, home sites, and so on, plus a modest harvest of wood as well.

SUGGESTED READING LIST

GENERAL

BARNETT, L. (ed.), 1955. *The world we live in.* New York: Simon and Schuster.

BATES, MARSTON, 1960. *The forest and the sea.* New York: Random House.

BOURLIÈRE, F., and others, 1957. *The tropics.* New York: Knopf.

BROWN, HARRISON, BONNER, J., and WIER, J., 1957. *The next 100 years.* New York: Viking.

GRAHAM, EDWARD H., 1944. *Natural principles of land use.* New York: Oxford University Press.

KENDEIGH, S. CHARLES, 1961. *Animal ecology.* Englewood Cliffs, N.J.: Prentice-Hall. Chapter 22–28.

LEOPOLD, ALDO, 1941, "Lakes in relation to terrestrial life patterns." In *A Symposium on hydrobiology.* Madison: University of Wisconsin Press. Pp. 17–22.

ODUM, EUGENE P., 1959. *Fundamentals of ecology,* 2d ed. Philadelphia: Saunders. Section II, pp. 289–418; Section III, pp. 419–451.

POLUNIN, NICHOLAS, 1960. *Introduction to plant geography.* New York: McGraw-Hill.

THOMAS, W. L. (ed.), 1956. *Man's role in changing the face of the earth.* Chicago: University of Chicago Press.

THE SEAS

CARSON, RACHEL, 1952. *The sea around us.* New York: Oxford University Press.

COKER, R. E., 1947. *This great and wide sea.* Chapel Hill: University of North Carolina Press.

CROMIE, W. J., 1960. *Exploring the secrets of the sea.* Englewood Cliffs, N.J.: Prentice-Hall.

HARDY, A. C., *The open sea.* I: *The world of plankton* (1956); II: *Fish and fisheries* (1959). London: Collins.

SEARS, MARY (ed.), 1961. *Oceanography.* Washington, D.C.: American Association for the Advancement of Science, Publication No. 67.

SPILHAUS, ATHELSTAN, 1959. *Turn to the sea.* Washington, D.C.: National Academy of Sciences-National Research Council. (Free pamphlet describing opportunities in oceanography.)

Many beautifully illustrated articles on the sea have appeared in *Scientific American*. The following are of special ecological interest: "Food from the sea" (October 1949); "Deep sea life" (August 1951, July 1952, and July 1957); "Voyage of the Challenger" (May 1953); "Underwater television" (June 1953); "The Peru current" (March 1954); "The circulation of the ocean" (September 1955); "Sargasso sea" (January 1955); "Sharks vs men" (June 1957); "The bathyscape" (April 1958); "Carbon dioxide and climate" (July 1959); "The Arctic ocean" (May 1961); "Salps" (January 1961); "Oceanic life of Antarctic" (September 1962); "Deep scattering layers" (August 1962).

ESTUARIES AND SEASHORES

BROWN, FRANK A., "Biological clocks and the fiddler crab," *Scientific American,* April 1954, pp. 34–37.

CARSON, RACHEL, 1955. *The edge of the sea.* Boston: Houghton Mifflin. (Also in Mentor paperback edition.)

INGLE, ROBERT M., "The life of an estuary," *Scientific American,* May 1954, pp. 64–69.

KORRINGA, PETER, "Oysters," *Scientific American,* November 1953, pp. 86–92.

ODUM, EUGENE P., "The role of tidal marshes in estuarine production," *The Conservationist,* June-July 1961, pp. 12–15.

PEARSE, A. S., HUMM, H. J., and WARTON, G. W., "Ecology of sand beaches at Beaufort, N.C.," *Ecological Monographs,* Vol. 12 (1942), pp. 136–190.

STEPHENSON, T. A., and STEPHENSON, ANNE, "The universal features of zonation between tide-marks on rocky coasts," *Journal of Ecology,* Vol. 37 (1949), pp. 289–305.

YONGE, C. M., 1949. *The sea shore.* London: Collins (New Naturalist Series).

FRESH WATER

BENNETT, G. W., 1962. *Management of artificial lakes and ponds.* New York: Reinhold.

COKER, R. E., 1954. *Lakes, streams, and ponds.* Chapel Hill: University of North Carolina Press.

DEEVEY, EDWARD S., "Life in the depths of a pond," *Scientific American,* April 1951, pp. 68–72.

ERRINGTON, PAUL L., 1957. *Of men and marshes.* New York: Macmillan.

HYNES, H. B. N., 1962. *The biology of polluted waters.* Liverpool, Eng.: Liverpool University Press.

MACAN, T. T., and WORTHINGTON, E. B., 1951. *Life in lakes and rivers.* London: Collins (New Naturalist Series).

REID, GEORGE K., 1961. *Ecology of inland waters and estuaries.* New York: Reinhold.

RUTTNER, FRANZ, 1953. *Fundamentals of limnology.* Toronto: University of Toronto Press.

DESERTS

JAEGER, E. C., 1957. *The North American deserts.* Palo Alto, Calif.: Stanford University Press.

LEOPOLD, A. STARKER, 1961. *The desert.* New York: Time, Inc. (Life Nature Library).

SCHMIDT-NIELSEN, B., and SCHMIDT-NIELSEN, K., "The water economy of desert mammals," *Scientific Monthly,* Vol. 69 (1949), pp. 180–185. (See also "Physiology of the camel," *Scientific American,* December 1959, pp. 140–151.

WENT, FRITS, "The ecology of desert plants," *Scientific American,* April 1955, pp. 68–75.

TUNDRA

BLISS, L. C., "A comparison of plant development in microenvironments of arctic and alpine tundras," *Ecological Monographs,* Vol. 26 (1956), pp. 303–337.

ELTON, CHARLES, 1942. *Voles, mice and lemmings.* New York: Oxford University Press.

LEY, WILEY, 1962. *The poles.* New York: Time, Inc. (Life Nature Library).

SHELFORD, V. E., and TWOMEY, A. C., "Tundra animal communities in the vicinity of Churchill, Manitoba," *Ecology,* Vol. 22 (1941), pp. 47–69.

GRASSLANDS

CARPENTER, J. R., "The grassland biome," *Ecological Monographs,* Vol. 10 (1940), pp. 617–684.

DARLING, F. FRASER, "Wildlife husbandry in Africa," *Scientific American,* November 1960, pp. 123–134.

HANSON, H. C., "Ecology of the grassland," *Botanical Reviews*, Vol. 16 (1950), pp. 283–360.

SEARS, PAUL B., 1935. *Deserts on the march*. Norman: University of Oklahoma Press.

WEAVER, J. E., 1954. *North American prairie*. 1956. *Grasslands of the Great Plains* (co-author, F. W. Albertson). Johnsen Publ. Co., Lincoln, Nebraska.

FORESTS

BRAUN, E. LUCY, 1950. *Deciduous forests of eastern North America*. Philadelphia: McGraw-Hill-Blakiston.

FARB, PETER, 1961. *The forest*. New York: Time, Inc. (Life Nature Library).

McCORMICK, JACK, 1959. *The living forest*. New York: Harper.

RICHARD, P. W., 1952. *The tropical rain forest*. New York: Cambridge University Press.

SHELFORD, V. E., and OLSON, S., "Sere, climax and influent animals with special reference to the transcontinental coniferous forest of North America," *Ecology*, Vol. 16 (1935), pp. 375–402.

WHITTAKER, R. H., "Vegetation in the Great Smoky Mountains," *Ecological Monographs*, Vol. 26 (1956), pp. 1–80.

INDEX

INDEX

Numbers in **boldface type** indicate pages on which terms and concepts are most fully defined or explained. Only names of persons not accompanied by specific literature reference are indexed. Place names are not indexed.

143